大师经典文库

Sir Thomas More

乌 托 邦
Utopia

托马斯·莫尔　著

Ralph Robinson　译

外语教学与研究出版社

(京)新登字 155 号

京权图字 01－97－1109

图书在版编目(CIP)数据

乌托邦：英文／(英)莫尔 (More, T.) 著. －北京：外语教学与
研究出版社, 1997.9
(大师经典文库)
ISBN 7－5600－1362－7

Ⅰ.乌…　Ⅱ.莫…　Ⅲ.英语－语言读物　Ⅳ. H319.4:D

中国版本图书馆 CIP 数据核字(97)第 24284 号

大师经典文库

乌托邦

托马斯·莫尔　著

Ralph Robinson　译

＊　＊　＊

外语教学与研究出版社出版发行
(北京西三环北路 19 号　100089)
http://www.fltrp.com.cn
北京国防印刷厂印刷
开本 850×1168　1/32　5 印张
1998 年 4 月第 1 版　2000 年 8 月第 3 次印刷
印数：30001—40000 册

＊　＊　＊

ISBN 7－5600－1362－7
H·769
定价：5.90 元
如有印刷、装订质量问题出版社负责调换

The paper in this book is produced from pure wood
pulp,without the use of chlorine or any other substance
harmful to the environment.The energy used in its
production consists almost entirely of hydroelectricity
and heat generated from waste material,thereby
conserving fossil fuels and contributing little
to the greenhouse effect

This edition published 1997 byWordsworth Editions Limited
Cumberland House,Crib Street,Ware,Hertfordshire SG12 9ET

ISBN 1 85326 474 1

© Wordsworth Editions Limited 1997

Wordsworth® is a registered trade mark of
Wordsworth Editions Ltd

Typeset in Great Britain by Antony Gray
Printed and bound in Denmark by Nørhaven

出版说明

我社自90年代以来，一直以促进国际文化交流为己任，致力于原版外语著作的引进和出版工作，逐步形成了规模化、系列化、精品化的出版传统，在广大读者中产生了一定的影响。但是，目前我国外语图书出版呈现出较为严重的不均衡局面，即文艺类图书品种相对齐全，而人文科学、社会科学类外语图书的出版却寥寥可数，远远滞后于日益增长的文化市场需求。为了填补这一空白，我社编辑出版了这套英文版哲学、社会科学类丛书"大师经典文库"，系统地推出一批世界著名思想家、哲学家、历史学家、心理学家的经典学术名著，包括我国古代哲学籍典的权威英译本，为广大英语学习者提供高质量的阅读文本，也为各类社会科学研究工作者提供必备的学术资料。本丛书每一种均由著名专家、学者撰写评介性的序言。

外语教学与研究出版社

1997 年 11 月

序　言

　　托马斯·莫尔 (Thomas More, 1478 — 1535) 是英国早期空想社会主义的主要代表，欧洲文艺复兴时期的文学家和政治活动家，杰出的人道主义者。1478年2月7日生于伦敦一个较为富裕的家庭，用莫尔自己的话来说，它"名声虽然不大，却是一个正直的家庭"。其父约翰·莫尔曾任英国皇家高等刑事法庭法官，甚至还受到了国王爱德华四世的器重，曾获得过贵族爵位。莫尔早年受到过良好的教育，他还在孩提时代，就被送入伦敦的圣安东尼学校。在那里，他就几乎熟练地掌握了拉丁文。13岁 (1491) 那一年，由于其父的关系，他寄住在坎特伯雷红衣大主教莫顿的家中。莫顿这位具有政治家和大法官等多重身份的博学长者给少年莫尔留下了深刻的印象和愉快的回忆。1492 年，14岁的莫尔进入牛津大学，继续攻读和深造拉丁文和形式逻辑。在此期间，他大量广泛地研读了古代希腊罗马学者的哲学著作，并深受希腊大哲柏拉图和亚里士多德思想的影响，尤其是柏拉图的《理想国》对其后来思想的发展产生了至关重要的影响。此后，即于1496 年，他又转而攻读法律，1497年结识了荷兰人文主义者D·伊拉斯谟，并在以后的岁月中与其建立了深厚的友谊，1501 年成为正式律师。作为一个公正无私的法官和穷人的庇护者，莫尔受到了公众的敬爱。伊拉斯谟在谈到莫尔在法律界出色的工作和廉洁奉公、为人正直的品格时这样说道：他"毫不悭吝，也不贪财"，无论什么时候"也不拒绝任何人的友好诚挚的建议，关心他人的利益比关心自己为重"，而且，这些美好的品格一直保持到他当了法官的时候，均丝毫未变，在那时，"无论谁也没有像莫尔那样审理过这么多的案件，无论谁也没有比他更为光明磊落地处理这些案件，"在大多数情况下，他宁可自己蒙受损失，而"降低诉讼人因立案照例应支付的费用……莫尔的这些品德使他赢得了同胞们的最大爱戴"。①1504 年，26 岁的莫尔当选为英国议会下院议员，1509 年，亨利八世继位后，莫尔历任国家要职，1923 年，当选下院议长。1529 年被国王任命为大法官。莫尔在亨利八世刚继位之初，曾对这位新国王寄予厚望，他也曾和许多英国朋友们为新国王的继位而激动、兴奋过，欢呼雀跃过，然而，后来的情形却使他们大失所望。莫尔由于对亨利八世的宗教政策提出异议，拒绝承认国王在教会的领袖地位，此外，作为大法官，他对国王的离婚案亦提出了异议，故于 1532 年不得不辞去大法官职务。1534 年，他被诬陷入狱，1535 年 7 月 6 日以"叛国罪"被处以极刑，莫尔因此成了亨利八世心胸偏狭与暴政的牺牲品。就莫尔的死而言，他是不幸的，但就莫尔一生的思想贡献而言，他又是伟大的、不朽的。就在莫尔死后 400 年，1935 年，他重新被世人追谥为圣徒。他的英名又被列入前苏联莫斯科红场石碑上的革命英雄名单。英国天主教辩护士 G·K·切斯特顿认为，莫尔堪称英国历史上的伟人。在今天英国的威斯敏斯特大厦和伦敦塔均有他的纪念碑。

莫尔只活了 57 岁。在他 57 年的生涯中，他无疑为人类的进步作出了不可磨灭的贡献。他的那部未来得及完成的《国王理查三世的历史》（约 1513—1518）一书，是人们公认的英国编史工作的第一部杰作。1516 年，莫尔的代表作《乌托邦》出版，在这部惊世之作中，作者对当时欧洲各国尤其是对英国的普遍经济状况和社会环境进行了深刻的分析，对当时这些国家的政治制度和社会制度进行了严厉的批判和控诉，并提出了私有制是一切社会罪恶的根源的观点，指出英国"圈地运动"的后果是出现了一个"羊吃人"的社会。莫尔描绘了一个没有剥削、没有压迫、没有欺诈、没有私有财产和贫富差异的理想社会，并提出了一系列诸

<hr />

① 参见《伊拉斯谟书信集》(Opus Epistolarum Des. Roterodami)，H·M·艾伦编辑，第五集，第 1 章，牛津 1958 年版。

如人人劳动、按需分配、助人为乐、人人平等的理想和原则。莫尔的这些空想社会主义的原则和理想为后来科学社会主义的产生和形成提供了基础和条件。下面，我们就莫尔《乌托邦》一书的基本内容和特征对莫尔空想社会主义思想作一简要的叙述。

《乌托邦①》一书初版于1516年的比利时卢万城，用拉丁文撰写而成。据说，在经过了四个半世纪之多的今天，该书的初版珍本举世共知的仅有五部，其中的一部为前苏联的马克思恩格斯列宁学院所珍藏。

莫尔的《乌托邦》以对话的形式，反映了早期无产阶级对资本主义原始积累时期残酷剥削和压榨的强烈抗议，同时描绘了作者的理想社会，对以后社会主义思想的发展有很大的影响。我们有时提到的所谓"乌托邦的社会主义"，其名称的来源即在于此。在莫尔的理想社会中，私有制被废除，劳动产品全归社会所有，公民在政治上一律平等，人人参加劳动。但由于时代和阶级的局限，这个理想的社会是以农业和手工业生产为基础的，而且还有奴隶的存在。在教育上，他主张儿童都应受初等教育，教学都应用本族语进行，并提出劳动教育的主张。在哲学上，莫尔崇尚伊壁鸠鲁的思想，相信人的认识来源于经验，但他往往以唯理论的观点反对经院哲学和宗教迷信，而不完全否定宗教，故在乌托邦中仍有宗教存在。

莫尔的乌托邦思想不是凭空捏造的，它是人类社会历史发展到了一定阶段的必然产物。我们知道，早在莫尔之前很久，尖锐的社会矛盾就已存在，尤其是社会的贫富悬殊和人与人之间的阶级差别以及由之造成的不平等现象，使人类之间的敌对斗争尖锐化、复杂化。因此，通过一种什么样的途径、方式或手段来摆脱这种社会矛盾，消除人类之间的敌对状态和残酷斗争，一直是有

---

① "乌托邦"一词由希腊文的"否"和"地方"这两个词义所构成，意即"虚无之乡"。后来这个词成了通用词。莫尔《乌托邦》一书的书名最初是Nusqama (由拉丁文nusquam，意即"无处"一词而来)。"乌托邦"这个标题最初出现在1516年11月12日给伊拉斯谟的信中。

识之士和进步思想家们所关注和思考的焦点。正如列宁曾经指出过的那样：“许多世纪以来，甚至几千年来，人类早已幻想过‘立即’消灭所有一切剥削。”① 因此，在英国早期的资本主义原始积累时期，莫尔亲眼所见的是农民大批地失去土地和家园，劳动者由于被残酷地剥夺而变得极度贫困这样一种社会现状。面对着这种社会现状，他开始对“消灭所有一切剥削，建立人人幸福平等”问题的思考就不足为奇了。《乌托邦》一书的写作动因，首先来自于当时英国由于资本主义关系而导致的激烈的社会冲突。写作的原料或素材当然也来自于组成当时社会现实的各个方面，其中包括政治、经济、社会、文化教育和宗教、道德、法律等等；其次，由于受古代希腊哲学家柏拉图《理想国》思想的影响，莫尔早在青年时代就已十分推崇柏拉图的《理想国》，并且常常是废寝忘食地研读它，爱不释手。伊拉斯谟在致乌尔里赫·冯·胡滕的一封信中曾这样说道：莫尔酷爱“柏拉图关于公有制的学说”，并千方百计地捍卫了它。② 莫尔早期的传记作家斯塔普莱顿也在其著中论证了柏拉图思想对莫尔思想的影响，他说：莫尔“最喜欢阅读和研究柏拉图以及柏拉图派哲学家的著作，因为，从他们的著作中能够了解到关于国家管理、公民的社会生活以及他们相互关系的许多事情”。③ 我们可以在《乌托邦》中找到柏拉图的《理想国》对莫尔思想影响的痕迹。④

莫尔《乌托邦》一书中的空想社会主义思想的展开，主要是从对当时英国社会—经济发展现状的批判入手的。首先，莫尔对英国“羊吃人”的圈地运动作了全面的调查、分析和批判。《乌托邦》中所提供的有关文献资料反映了16世纪的英国在经营农业的方式方面所发生的历史性变化：原先那些对耕种其世袭领地

---

① 列宁：《小资产阶级的社会主义和无产阶级的社会主义》，《列宁全集》第9卷，人民出版社1959年版，第431页。
②③④ 参见奥西诺夫斯基：《托马斯·莫尔传》，商务印书馆1984年版，第105页。

的农民进行剥削的封建领主已不再满足于获得传统的地租。随着市场情况的变化，许多英国封建主开始抛弃原有那种需要劳动力较多而收入较少的土地经营方式，转而经营大规模的牧羊业。正是由于牧羊业的迅速发展，导致了大规模的圈地运动和对农民的掠夺，流离失所、漂泊无定的农民成了大地主暴力的牺牲品，整个社会顿时显得更加混乱、黑暗和残酷。莫尔在书中怀着十分沉痛的心情描绘了把耕地变为大牧场给人民带来的悲惨后果以及大地主圈地者的残暴和不人道，他说：这些贪得无厌的剥夺者们"把可以居住可以耕种的每个角落都弄成荒地，仿佛他们的鸟囿和兽园占地还不够大"。① 莫尔爱憎分明，他对那些被无辜剥夺家园而实际是"全部财富的创造者"的农民和手工业者们深表同情，而对那些圈地者怀着深刻的憎恨，把他们斥之为"寄生虫"，一种"馋嘴而且是贪婪的国蠹"，② 他们"破坏地界，用一条篱栅圈起几千亩土地。佃农们从土地上被逐出，他们的财产被用诡计或压制的方式剥夺掉。他们受尽折磨，不得不出卖自己的家业"。③ 由于人们为了生计而不得不被迫出卖自己一切值钱的家业，一旦他们在流浪中钱花尽后，在叫天天不应、呼地地不灵的走投无路的情况下，又不得不被迫走上诸如抢劫、盗窃为生的犯罪之路，有的甚至因此而受到绞刑等的惩处。总之，圈地运动使千千万万的男人和女人、丈夫和妻子、孤儿和寡母走上了悲惨绝望的境地。

当然，圈地运动也并不是造成当时英国普遍灾难性贫困的唯一原因。在《乌托邦》的第一部，莫尔通过杰出人物拉斐尔·希斯拉德之口指出了造成这种普遍灾难性贫困的另外两个原因：一是战争；二是统治者腐败的寄生性生活。

---

① 转引自奥西诺夫斯基：《托马斯·莫尔传》，商务印书馆1984年版，第113页。
②③ 转引自奥西诺夫斯基：《托马斯·莫尔传》，商务印书馆1984年版，第114页。

亨利七世和亨利八世统治期间，频繁的、旷日持久的连年战争不但耗尽国力，而且民不聊生。战争造成了千百万少胳膊缺腿的病残者，这些曾经为响应国家和国王号召而浴血疆场的人们，病残的躯体使他们再也不能从事正常的劳作，健康因素和年龄状况都不可能使他们有重新获得学习、掌握新技术、谋求新职业的机会和条件，等待着他们的无疑是贫困、饥饿、衰老和死亡。这些人既是社会和时代的牺牲品，同时又成了社会的包袱和不安定因素。

此外，统治者们腐败和不劳而获的寄生性生活，更是造成社会不平等现象的主要因素。他们对广大老百姓进行敲骨吸髓的重重盘剥，他们的生活穷奢极欲、挥霍无度。极大的社会反差致使一些人过着花天酒地、醉生梦死的生活，另一些人走投无路，铤而走险，沦为流浪汉、乞丐、小偷或强盗(其中自然也有因不平而豁出性命为之的举刀杀人犯)。《乌托邦》第一部十分深刻地揭示出了导致英国社会普遍灾难性贫困的三大原因，的确是切中了社会之时弊的。当时英国社会所面临的主要问题就是人与人之间的不平等。那么，如何能消除或摆脱这种不平等呢?这更是莫尔《乌托邦》一书所关注的主题。

《乌托邦》不但对产生(包括普遍性贫困在内的)社会灾难的原因进行了深刻的揭示和分析，同时还指出了种种恶习(如不平等、剥削、农民和手工业者等劳动大众的赤贫以及对下层劳苦大众血腥立法等现象)得以产生的基本根源就在于私有制。针对这种私有制统治，莫尔指出："凡是有私有制，凡是人们用金钱衡量一切的地方就会有这种统治，那么，对国家的管理未必有一天能够是公正和成功的，"[①] 如果有谁面对着这样的统治而承认这样的社会是公正的，那就无异于承认"最坏的人获得一切美好的东西是正确的"，[②] 或者说承认一切财富由极少数人瓜分，其

---

①②参见奥西诺夫斯基：《托马斯·莫尔传》，商务印书馆1984年版，第119页。

他人同时一贫如洗、饥寒交迫是可取的。① 莫尔看到了私有制统治的恶果必然是创造财富的劳动者不能拥有财富，劳动者创造出来的财富必然被私有制的统治者（即"社会上最坏的那部分人"）所攫取。因此，莫尔认为，只有消灭私有制，财富的分配才能公平合理，人们也才有可能过安宁无忧的日子。相反，如果私有制存在，那么，人类的绝大多数人将永遭贫穷和苦难。照这样下去，复兴社会并使它日益完善美好也将是没有任何指望的。这就是莫尔要消灭私有制的基本理由。

莫尔在《乌托邦》的第二部中，着重对他那个消灭了私有制和不平等的理想社会进行了详细、具体、生动的描绘。首先，他想到的是如何治理国家，从而使之有利于公众的社会福利事业。莫尔乌托邦理想社会的基本制度是实行财产公有。国家为了全社会的利益，一些生活必需品由元老院来负责统计和支配。这个社会之所以物质丰富，其原因就是：一、没有个人财产私有制；二、人人都必须参加生产劳动，社会上没有游手好闲之徒，每一个人除了从事农业劳动外，还必须要学会一门或多门手艺。这样，劳动，就不再会出现过寄生性生活的人了。参加创造财富的人多了，社会的物质就自然会极大地丰富，在这个基础上，按需分配的原则就可以实现。

由于实行了人人劳动和按需分配的原则，因此，货币的功能也就随之丧失。金钱用不着了，人们也就不贪金钱了。莫尔说：在乌托邦取消货币的使用，"这就砍掉了多少烦恼啊！这就铲除了多少罪恶啊！谁不知道，金钱既然取消，欺骗、盗窃、抢劫、吵架、骚乱、喧闹、叛乱、暗杀、变节、放毒等虽然每天受到惩罚却只能施以打击而不能制止的罪行，就不发生了？谁又不知道，恐惧、焦虑、烦恼、辛苦的操作、不眠的通宵也会随着金钱的消失而消失？而且，贫穷的手仅仅由缺乏金钱造成，一旦金钱到处废

---

① 参见奥西诺夫斯基：《托马斯·莫尔传》，商务印书馆1984年版，第119页。

除，贫穷也就马上减少以至消失了。"① 金钱是财产或财富的象征，对金钱的占有就是对财产或财富的拥有。金钱是万恶之源，多少人的苦难和多少人的犯罪以及社会的不安定都与金钱有关。因此，乌托邦社会经济制度的基本特征就是取消金钱制。金钱制的取消从制度上铲除了私有制的基础，从而从根本上割除了一大社会毒瘤。

在《乌托邦》中，莫尔除对未来理想社会的经济制度作了描绘外，他还对未来新国家的社会政治制度作了具体的构想。

乌托邦是一个由诸多城市组成的联邦。这些联邦直接管辖下的城市，其法律和设施均是相同的，首都设在西马乌鲁提城，元老院是国家的主要政治机构，其成员均由各个城市每年选派出来的人员所组成，任期一年。除了元老院外，还有一个民众大会，此乃与元老院并存的国家政治机构。国家政治管理机构的管理方式完全是公开性的，换言之，它是在全民的监督下进行的，因此，带有极高的透明度。其中还规定：共和国的高级行政官员必须从博学多才的学者中挑选。只有由深明事理的哲学家和学者来领导，才能"把粗野、不文明的人民引到那种迄今还优越于几乎所有凡人的生活方式和文明"。② 在乌托邦中，不但国家的官吏富有学识，清正廉明，而且，他们与民众也始终保持一种密切的友好关系。在那里，官员们工作不怠惰，态度不傲慢，丝毫不会有令人望而生畏之感，百姓们因此也乐意把他们视为"父母"，由衷地尊敬他们，爱戴他们。国家官员与人民大众的这种鱼水相依、水乳交融的关系和废除了私有制与特权阶层的人与人之间的平等关系以及民主政治制度的切实实行，使我们当代人似乎真正从中感悟或想象到：在那样一种理想社会中，一个个挺立着的都是不受任何压迫、剥削、欺诈的自由人民和昂首挺胸、掌握了自己命运的真正的主人。

---

① 托马斯·莫尔：《乌托邦》，商务印书馆1982年版，第117页。
② 《莫尔全集》，第4卷，第122页。

乌托邦人酷爱自由，反对暴政，热爱民主，憎恨专制。他们也希望邻国的人民像他们一样过上幸福安宁的生活。因此，他们也常常应邀派出一些人员去邻国当官员，按照乌托邦的管理模式进行管理。由此可见，乌托邦社会的人们已经具有了那种不仅要使本国人民获得幸福和解放，而且还要让他人或他国人民获得幸福和解放的宽阔胸怀和远大理想。

　　乌托邦不但是一个官民平等、互尊互爱、亲密无间、共享幸福的民主国家，同时也是一个高度重视法制的国家。乌托邦人深深懂得法制能保护人民大众的利益。法律能使他们幸福安宁地生活，法律能给他们带来人与人之间的种种平等。因此，自觉地学法、守法、用法成了公民的自觉意识和行为。乌托邦的法律并不繁杂，一切法律条文的制订都以普通老百姓能看懂为前提。在那里，没有所谓"含混不清"的法律条文，所以，一般的老百姓理解和掌握并不难。在乌托邦人看来，任何公正的法律，都是简单而又明了的。越简单越明了的法律就越为广大人民所学习和掌握，而一个人人懂得法制和人人掌握法律的社会就必定是安宁幸福的社会。由于乌托邦人人人都懂法、守法，因此，在那里，律师职业就成为多余的了。

　　在对外政治和战争问题上，乌托邦人主张国与国之间应该和睦共处，相安无事，不应该发生冲突和战争。乌托邦人崇尚和平，厌恶战争。他们认为，战争是一种极野蛮的行为，没有比通过战争赢得的荣誉更不光彩的了。不过，乌托邦人反对战争，但他们又不怕战争。如果一旦有战争，他们也同样可以在不得已的情况下接受战争的挑战，因此，莫尔说："他们的男女在固定的日子里刻苦地参加军训，锻炼自己，唯恐一旦有需要而他们不能作战。但是他们决不轻易地投入战争。他们出战仅仅是为了保护本国领土，或驱除侵入友邦的敌人，或出于怜悯某个受专制压迫的民族而用武力把他们从暴君的桎梏奴役下解放出来，这是人类的同情心所激起的一种行动。"[①]　由此可见，乌托邦人在对外政策和战争

---

　　① 托马斯·莫尔:《乌托邦》，商务印书馆1982年版，第94页。

问题上的看法是：主张国与国之间的和睦友好和平等，但如果有战争，他们一是反对，二是不怕。一旦打起仗来，也决不手软。乌托邦人决不首先发动战争，但他们也随时准备给外来入侵者或侵略友邦的敌人以迎头痛击。不过，他们在介入战争时，尽量不让战争在本国进行，即使是在他国进行，也尽量做到不伤害广大人民，决不滥杀平民和无辜。乌托邦人的这种不要战争，不怕战争，为正义而战和为国家、为人类的和平幸福而战、战而胜之的英勇无畏精神，仍是我们今天的人们所应学习的。

莫尔在《乌托邦》中还论及了宗教问题。乌托邦人有其自己的意识形态。莫尔认为，国家应该实行宗教宽容，允许每个公民有宗教信仰自由。在乌托邦岛的每个城市，都有各种各样的宗教。一些信奉者都各有自己的崇拜之神，如有人崇拜日神，有人崇拜月神，有的崇拜星辰，有的则将以往历史上某个为人所尊崇或爱戴的圣贤奉为神明。不过，在乌托邦岛上持上述信仰的只是一小部分，而对于绝大多数人或者说对于那些较有见识的人来说，他们不信上述这些神灵，"而只信某个单一的神，这个神是不为人知的，永恒的，巨大无边的，奥妙无穷的，远远超出人类悟解的，就其威力说而不是就其形体说是充塞宇宙间的。他们称他为父，把万物的起源、生长、发育、演化、老死都归之于他。只有对他，乌托邦人才加以神的尊称……并且其他所有的乌托邦人尽管信仰不一，却在这点上意见一致，即只有一个至高的神，是全世界的创造者和真主宰，在本国语言中一致称为'密特拉①'"。②无论是一神信仰还是多神信仰，在乌托邦社会中都是不受干涉的。乌托邦人崇尚信仰自由，故即使是对于其教义不为乌托邦人所赞成的基督教来说，他们也还是持"既不阻止别人信从，也不侵犯已经信从的人"的态度，③乌托邦人历来就有一条最古的制度，那就是："任何人不能由于自己的信仰而受到责罚。"，④这也许

---

① 密特拉 (Mythras) 即古代波斯的太阳神。

② 托马斯·莫尔：《乌托邦》，商务印书馆1982年版，第103页。

③④ 托马斯·莫尔：《乌托邦》，商务印书馆1982年版，第105页。

就是乌托邦人具有高度宗教信仰自由的重要历史原因吧。莫尔的乌托邦的宗教宽容精神与乌托邦的国家政治管理手段是有密切联系的。它是与理性主义精神有关的。在乌托邦国家，只要每个人的宗教信仰是积极的，就允许他持有这种信仰。乌托邦社会中的每一个人都可以不受阻碍地自由信奉适合其特性的宗教。不要小看宗教信仰自由，这里与国家的统治管理水平有着极大的关系。甚至可以说，宗教信仰自由有利于国家的统治。美国的乔·奥·赫茨勒在谈到乌托邦的宗教信仰与社会秩序的关系时这样写道：“乌托邦的每一个人都可以不受阻碍地信仰适合其特性的宗教。理性这个仁政的唯一试金石证明没有别的规定比这更合理了。哪里不强迫人民信仰某种宗教或压制宗教，哪里就不用害怕派别斗争和由此而引起的反社会后果。”① 宗教宽容使乌托邦公民们按照自己的意志和特性自由地信奉他们心中的尊神。人们在精神上有了理想的寄托，就自然会胸襟开阔，心平气和，社会上就再也不会有不平之人起来反抗或作乱。这样的社会，一定是安宁和祥和的。这样的国家管理是理性的和成功的。乌托邦之所以要主张信仰自由和宗教宽容，其实也是为了国家的长治久安和人民的幸福安康，因此，它既是国家理性管理的重要组成部分，同时也是国家仁政的体现。

　　关于莫尔《乌托邦》一书中的主要思想，限于篇幅，我们大致就论述到这里。上文讲到，莫尔的乌托邦思想在相当大的程度上受启示于柏拉图的《理想国》，然而，尽管如此，他在许多方面仍与柏拉图不同，甚至可以说是在《理想国》的基础上有了新的否定、修正、演进和发展。例如，柏拉图的《理想国》要求他的统治阶级那部分人的财产和妻室归公，以此作为限制或摒弃个人主义本性、让这些统治者能专心致力于国家治理和公众福利事业的一种积极举措。莫尔与柏拉图不同的是，他不但要废除财产私有制，而且主张必须废除阶级的差别。只有废除了阶级差别，

---

　　① 乔·奥·赫茨勒：《乌托邦思想史》，商务印书馆1990年版，第140页。

"法律面前人人平等"才有实现的可能。此外，莫尔还在其他诸方面提出了与柏拉图不同的思考。记得著名德国哲学史家文德尔班曾将莫尔的《乌托邦》与柏拉图的《理想国》作了精细的对照和比较，并作了如是评述："莫尔以现实为对比所描绘的、在乌托邦岛上的完美的社会状况的理想蓝图，其主要轮廓是模拟柏拉图的理想国。然而，这种人本主义的复活带有近代社会主义的色彩，它与原型不同之处在于废除了阶级差异：〔据那位古代思想家看来，在他思考现实存在的个人的智力和道德地位的差异之后，他认为阶级似乎是必然的了。〕它所效法的与其说是柏拉图的《理想国》，倒不如说是柏拉图的'规律'。莫尔从所有公民在法律面前人人平等的思想出发，为了尔后的发展，进行了典范的抽象工作；莫尔认为一切公民有权参加社团，而柏拉图的理想国则认为这些社团是对统治阶级的要求，把参加社团当作扬弃个人利益的本能的方法。在柏拉图那里，特权阶级应扬弃一切私有财产以便全心全意奉献于全民福利；而在莫尔那里，则要求把废除私有财产当作消除罪恶的最可靠的方法。废除私有财产是基于对公有财产人人有份的平等权利。但是与此同时，这位近代的乌托邦主义者还坚持那位古代哲学家的理想模型，坚持到了这样的程度，以至于认为对物质利益的绝对平分是所有公民同等享受社会、科学、艺术、精神财富的不可缺少的基础。的确不错，这位英国大臣比起那位雅典革新家来，在这方面，思想民主得多，并给予个人更大的私人生活的自由：莫尔决不会让全体公民限制在共同的信条和信念上。国家的公共设施就其有效的正常秩序而言基本上是针对外部生活事务的。他认为，要满足社会的物质需要，对于全社会成员，六小时的正常工作日就足够了，剩下的时间每一个人可以自由支配，去做更高尚的工作。在莫尔那里，根据这些规定，产生了出自柏拉图的蓝图、更高级形式的近代社会主义的纲领。"① 文德尔班的以上述评揭示了《理想国》与《乌托邦》的源流关系，又阐

---

　　① 文德尔班：《哲学史教程》下卷，商务印书馆1993年版，第588页。

明了这二者之间的思想之异同，既承认了柏拉图《理想国》的历史地位，又肯定了莫尔《乌托邦》源于《理想国》又高于《理想国》的历史进步意义。

　　莫尔，作为一名空想社会主义者，比柏拉图这位古代哲人要高明得多。莫尔不愧是一位高瞻远瞩的思想家，他始终站在时代的高度，以其深邃的洞察力，预见到了人类社会发展的美好远景和精神走向。早在16世纪资本主义原始积累时期，作为一个资产阶级学者，莫尔以一种超前的意识预示着人类未来发展的曙光，从而给迷茫的人类以理性的启示。莫尔的乌托邦思想对人类的发展产生了持久而深远的影响。莫尔不仅是一个人道主义者，而且，他更是一位卓越的思想家。他写《乌托邦》，并不是像一般作家那样凭空臆想或从其他作品中寻求资料。相反，他从资本原始积累时期的英国现实社会中发现问题，寻找答案。作者在书中充满着对当时社会中的黑暗面(诸如对农民的残酷剥削，统治者的贪婪、荒淫和寄生性等) 的无情揭露和批判，同时对下层劳动人民 (尤其是农民) 寄予深切的同情。这些都说明作为资产阶级学者的莫尔已经摆脱了资产阶级人道主义的局限。西方有的学者[①]，他们试图通过对《乌托邦》的诠释，把他与古希腊罗马和中世纪的思想混为一淡，以此阉割莫尔思想最本质的东西——共产主义理想。莫尔在对封建专制国家的政治制度进行无情批判的同时，早已看透了私有制是这种以剥削为特征的专制国家赖以存在的基础，并首次提出要消灭私有制，用一种没有私有制和没有人剥削人的制度来取代资产阶级制度。然而，由于历史的局限，莫尔这种空想共产主义者在提出这个理论之后，却无力去解决它。这正如恩格斯所说的，这种"不成熟的理论，是和不成熟的资本主义生产状况、不成熟的阶级状况相适应的。解决社会问题的办法还隐藏在不发达的经济关系中。"[②] 莫尔的最大历史功绩就在于他深刻地批判了当时业已产生的资产阶级制度，这正如列宁所指出的："当农

---

　　① 如别克尔、霍勒利斯、布里奇等。
　　② 恩格斯：《反杜林论》，《马克思恩格斯选集》第3卷，人民出版社1972　　298页。

15

奴制度被推翻而‘自由’资本主义社会出现的时候，立刻就暴露出一件事实，即这种自由意味着压迫和剥削劳动者的一种新制度。于是反映这种压迫并且表示反对这种压迫的各种社会主义学说就立刻产生了。”① 正是列宁所说的这种早期社会主义学说为科学社会主义理论的创立奠定了基础和条件。莫尔，作为空想共产主义的创始人，他的学说和集中体现这一学说的《乌托邦》理应受到我们今人的重视和厚爱，同时，我们也理应予以充分肯定和高度评价。

---

① 列宁：《马克思主义的三个来源和三个组成部分》，《列宁全集》第19卷，人民出版社1959年版，第7页。

Contents

Ralph Robinson to William Cecil   3

The Translator to the Gentle Reader   7
First Letter from Thomas More to Peter Giles   9
A Letter from Peter Giles to Jerome Busleyden   14
Second Letter from Thomas More to Peter Giles   17

THE FIRST BOOK:
Concerning the Best State of a Commonwealth   23

THE SECOND BOOK:
The Description of Utopia   59

    Of the Cities and namely of Amaurote   63
    Of the Magistrates   66
    Of Sciences, Crafts and Occupations   68
    Of their Living and Mutual Conversation Together   73
    Of their Journeying or Travelling Abroad   78
    Of Bondmen, Sick Persons, Wedlock, and
       divers other Matters   97
    Of Warfare   105
    Of the Religions in Utopia   114

A Metre of Four Verses in the Utopian Tongue   130
A Short Metre of Utopia   131
The Utopian Alphabet   132
Glossary   133
Names   135

UTOPIA

TO THE RIGHT HONOURABLE,AND HIS
VERY SINGULAR GOOD MASTER,

Master William Cecil, Esquire,

ONE OF THE TWO PRINCIPAL SECRETARIES TO
THE KING'S MOST EXCELLENT MAJESTY,
RALPH ROBINSON WISHETH CONTINUANCE OF HEALTH,
WITH DAILY INCREASE OF VIRTUE AND HONOUR

Upon a time, when tidings came to the city of Corinth that King Philip, father to Alexander surnamed the Great, was coming thitherward with an army royal to lay siege to the city, the Corinthians being forthwith stricken with great fear, began busily and earnestly to look about them, and to fall to work of all hands, some to scour and trim up harness, some to carry stones, some to amend and build higher the walls, some to rampire and fortify the bulwarks and fortresses, some one thing and some another, for the defending and strengthening of the city. The which busy labour and toil of theirs when Diogenes the philosopher saw, having no profitable business whereupon to set himself to work (neither any man required his labour and help as expedient for the commonwealth in that necessity), immediately girded about him his philosophical cloak, and began to roll and tumble up and down hither and thither upon the hillside, that lieth adjoining to the city, his great barrel or tun wherein he dwelt; for other dwelling-place would he have none.

This seeing, one of his friends, and not a little musing thereat, came to him: 'And I pray thee, Diogenes,' (quoth he) 'why doest thou thus, or what meanest thou hereby?' 'Forsooth I am tumbling my tub too, (quoth he) 'because it were no reason that I only should be idle where so many be working.'

In semblable manner, right honourable sir, though I be, as I am indeed, of much less ability than Diogenes was to do anything that shall or may be for the advancement and commodity of the public wealth of my native country; yet I, seeing every sort and kind of people in their vocation and degree busily occupied about the commonwealth's affairs; and especially learned men daily putting forth in writing new inventions and devices to the furtherance of the same; thought it my bounded duty to God, and to my country, so to tumble my tub, I mean so to occupy and exercise myself in bestowing such spare hours as I, being at the beck and commandment of others, could conveniently win to myself; that though no commodity of that my labour and travail to the public weal should arise, yet it might by this appear that mine endeavour and goodwill hereunto was not lacking.

To the accomplishment, therefore, and fulfilling of this my mind and purpose, I took upon me to turn and translate out of Latin into our English tongue the fruitful and profitable book which Sir Thomas More, knight, compiled and made of the new isle Utopia, containing and setting forth the best state and form of a public weal, a work (as it appeareth) written almost forty years ago by the said Sir Thomas More the author thereof. The which man, forasmuch as he was a man of late time, yea almost of these our days; and for the excellent qualities wherewith the great goodness of God had plentifully endowed him, and for the high place and room whereunto his prince had most graciously called him, notably well known, not only among us his countrymen, but also in foreign countries and nations; therefore I have not much to speak of him. This only I say: that it is much to be lamented of all, and not only of us Englishmen, that a man of so incomparable wit, of so profound knowledge, of so absolute learning, and of so fine eloquence, was yet nevertheless so much blinded, rather with obstinacy than with ignorance, that he could not, or rather would not, see the shining light of God's holy truth in certain principal points of Christian religion; but did rather choose to persevere and continue in his wilful and stubborn obstinacy even to the very death. This I say is a thing much to be lamented.

But letting this matter pass, I return again to *Utopia*, which (as I said before) is a work not only for the matter that it containeth, fruitful and profitable, but also for the writer's eloquent Latin style, pleasant and delectable. Which he that readeth in Latin, as the author himself wrote it, perfectly understanding the same, doubtless he shall take great pleasure and delight both in the sweet eloquence of the writer, and also in the witty invention and fine conveyance or disposition of the matter, but most of all in the good and wholesome lessons which be there in great plenty and abundance.

But now I fear greatly that in this my simple translation, through my rudeness and ignorance in our English tongue, all the grace and pleasure of the eloquence wherewith the matter in Latin is finely set forth may seem to be utterly excluded and lost; and therefore the fruitfulness of the matter itself much, peradventure, diminished and appaired. For who knoweth not, which knoweth anything, that an eloquent style setteth forth and highly commendeth a mean matter, whereas, on the other side, rude and unlearned speech defaceth and disgraceth a very good matter? According as I heard once a wise man say: A good tale evil told were better untold, and an evil tale well told needeth none other solicitor.

This thing I, well pondering and weighing with myself, and also knowing and knowledging the barbarous rudeness of my translation, was fully determined never to have put it forth in print, had it not been for certain friends of mine, and especially one, whom above all other I regarded, a man of sage and discreet wit, and in worldly matters by long use well experienced, whose name is George Tadlowe; an honest citizen of London, and in the same city well accepted and of good reputation; at whose request and instance I first took upon my weak and feeble shoulders the heavy and weighty burden of this great enterprise.

This man with divers other, but this man chiefly (for he was able to do more with me than many other), after that I had once rudely brought the work to an end, ceased not by all means possible continually to assault me, until he had at the last, what by the force of his pithy arguments and strong reasons, and what by his authority, so persuaded me, that he caused me to agree and consent to the imprinting hereof. He, therefore, as the chief persuader, must take upon him the danger which upon this bold and rash enterprise shall ensue. I, as I suppose, am herein clearly acquit and discharged of all blame.

Yet, honourable sir, for the better avoiding of envious and malicious tongues, I (knowing you to be a man, not only profoundly learned, and well affected towards all such as either can or will take pains in the well bestowing of that poor talent which God hath endued them with; but also for your godly disposition and virtuous qualities not unworthily now placed in authority and called to honour) am the bolder humbly to offer and dedicate unto your good mastership this my simple work; partly that under the safe conduct of your protection it may the better be defended from the obloquy of them which can say well by nothing that pleaseth not their fond and corrupt judgments, though it be else both fruitful and godly; and partly that by the means of this homely present I may the better renew and revive (which of late, as you know, I have already begun to do) that old acquaintance that was between you and me in the time of our childhood, being then schoolfellows together; not doubting that you for your native goodness and gentleness will accept in good part this poor gift, as an argument or token that mine old goodwill and hearty affection towards you is not, by reason of long tract of time and separation of our bodies, anything at all quailed and diminished, but rather (I assure you) much augmented and increased.

This, verily, is the chief cause that hath encouraged me to be so bold with your mastership. Else truly this my poor present is of such simple and mean sort, that it is neither able to recompense the least portion of your great gentleness to me, of my part undeserved, both in the time of our old acquaintance and also now lately again bountifully showed; neither yet fit and meet for the very baseness of it to be offered to one so worthy as you be. But Almighty God (who therefore ever be thanked) hath advanced you to such fortune and dignity, that you be of ability to accept thankfully as well a man's good will as his gift. The same God grant you and all yours long and joyfully to continue in all godliness and prosperity.

The Translator to the Gentle Reader

Thou shalt understand, gentle reader, that though this work of *Utopia* in English comes now the second time forth in print, yet was it never my mind nor intent that it should ever have been imprinted at all, as who for no such purpose took upon me at the first the translation thereof; but did it only at the request of a friend, for his own private use, upon hope that he would have kept it secret to himself alone. Whom though I knew to be a man indeed, both very witty and also skilful, yet was I certain that in the knowledge of the Latin tongue he was not so well seen as to be able to judge of the fineness or coarseness of my translation. Wherefore I went the more slightly through with it, propounding to myself therein rather to please my said friend's judgment than mine own. To the meanness of whose learning I thought it my part to submit and attemper my style. Lightly, therefore, I overran the whole work, and in short time, with more haste than good speed, I brought it to an end. But, as the Latin proverb sayeth: 'The hasty bitch bringeth forth blind whelps.' For when this my work was finished, the rudeness thereof showed it to be done in post-haste.

Howbeit, rude and base though it were, yet fortune so ruled the matter that to imprinting it came, and that partly against my will. Howbeit, not being able in this behalf to resist the pithy persuasions of my friends, and perceiving therefore none other remedy, but that forth it should, I comforted myself for the time only with this notable saying of Terence –

Ita vita est hominum, quasi quum ludas tesseris.
Si illud, quod est maxume opus iactu non cadit:
Illud, quod cecidit forte, id arte ut corrigas.

In which verses the poet likeneth or compareth the life of man to a dice-playing or a game at the tables: meaning therein, if that chance rise not which is most for the player's advantage, that then the chance, which fortune hath sent, ought so cunningly to be played, as may be to the player least damage. By the which worthy similitude surely the witty poet giveth us to understand, that though in any of our acts and doings (as oft chanceth) we happen to fail and miss of our good pretensed purpose, so that the success and our intent prove things far odd; yet so we ought with witty circumspection to handle the matter, that no evil or incommodity, as far forth as may be, and as in us lieth, do thereof ensue.

According to the which counsel, though I am indeed in comparison of an expert gamester and a cunning player but a very bungler, yet have I in this by chance, that on my side unawares hath fallen, so (I suppose) behaved myself that, as doubtless it might have been of me much more cunningly handled had I forethought so much or doubted any such sequel at the beginning of my play, so I am sure it had been much worse than it is if I had not in the end looked somewhat earnestly to my game. For though this work came not from me so fine, so perfect, and so exact yet at first, as surely for my small learning it should have done if I had then meant the publishing thereof in print; yet I trust I have now in this second edition taken about it such pains that very few great faults and notable errors are in it to be found. Now, therefore, most gentle reader, the meanness of this simple translation, and the faults that be therein (as I fear much there be some), I doubt not but thou wilt, in just consideration of the premises, gently and favourably wink at them. So doing thou shalt minister unto me good cause to think my labour and pains herein not altogether bestowed in vain. *Vale!*

Thomas More to Peter Giles Sendeth Greeting

I am almost ashamed, right well-beloved Peter Giles, to send unto
you this book of the Utopian commonwealth, well-nigh after a year's
space, which I am sure you looked for within a month and a half.
And no marvel. For you knew well enough that I was already
disburdened of all the labour and study belonging to the invention in
this work, and that I had no need at all to trouble my brains about the
disposition or conveyance of the matter; and therefore had herein
nothing else to do, but only to rehearse those things which you and I
together heard master Raphael tell and declare. Wherefore there was
no cause why I should study to set forth the matter with eloquence;
forasmuch as his talk could not be fine and eloquent, being first not
studied for, but sudden and unpremeditated, and then, as you know,
of a man better seen in the Greek language than in the Latin tongue.
And my writing, the nearer it should approach to his homely, plain,
and simple speech, so much the nigher should it go to the truth:
which is the only mark whereunto I do and ought to direct all my
travail and study herein.

I grant and confess, friend Peter, myself discharged of so much
labour, having all these things ready done to my hand, that almost
there was nothing left for me to do. Else either the invention or the
disposition of this matter might have required of a wit neither base,
neither at all unlearned, both some time and leisure, and also some
study. But if it were requisite and necessary that the matter should
also have been written eloquently, and not alone truly, of a surety
that thing could I have performed by no time nor study. But now
seeing all these cares, stays, and lets were taken away, wherein else so
much labour and study should have been employed, and that there
remained no other thing for me to do but only to write plainly the
matter as I heard it spoken; that indeed was a thing light and easy to
be done. Howbeit to the dispatching of this so little business, my

other cares and troubles did leave almost less than no leisure. While I
do daily bestow my time about law matters; some to plead, some to
hear, some as an arbitrator with mine award to determine, some as an
umpire or a judge with my sentence finally to discuss; while I go one
way to see and visit my friend, another way about mine own private
affairs; while I spend almost all the day abroad among others, and the
residue at home among mine own; I leave to myself, I mean to my
book, no time.

For when I am come home, I must commune with my wife, chat
with my children, and talk with my servants. All the which things I
reckon and account among business, forasmuch as they must of
necessity be done: and done must they needs be, unless a man will be
a stranger in his own house And in any wise a man must so fashion
and order his conditions, and so appoint and dispose himself, that he
be merry, jocund, and pleasant among them, whom either nature
hath provided, or chance hath made, or he himself hath chosen to be
the fellows and companions of his life; so that with too much gentle
behaviour and familiarity he do not mar them, and by too much
sufferance, of his servants make them his masters.

Among these things now rehearsed, stealeth away the day, the
month, the year. When do I write, then? And all this while have I
spoken no word of sleep, neither yet of meat, which among a great
number doth waste no less time than doth sleep, wherein almost half
the lifetime of man creepeth away. I therefore do win and get only
that time which I steal from sleep and meat. Which time, because it is
very little, and yet somewhat it is, therefore have I once at the last,
though it be long first, finished *Utopia*, and have sent it to you, friend
Peter, to read and peruse, to the intent that if anything have escaped
me, you might put me in remembrance of it. For though in this
behalf I do not greatly mistrust myself (which would God I were
somewhat in wit and learning, as I am not all of the worst and dullest
memory), yet have I not so great trust and confidence in it that I
think nothing could fall out of my mind.

For John Clement, my boy, who as you know was there present
with us, whom I suffer to be away from no talk wherein may be any
profit or goodness (for out of this young-bladed and new-shot-up
corn, which hath already begun to spring up both in Latin and Greek
learning, I look for plentiful increase at length of goodly ripe grain),
he I say hath brought me into a great doubt. For whereas Hythloday

(unless my memory fails me) said that the bridge of Amaurote, which goeth over the river of Anyder, is five hundred paces, that is to say, half a mile in length: my John sayeth that two hundred of those paces must be plucked away, for that the river containeth there not above three hundred paces in breadth. I pray you heartily call the matter to your remembrance. For if you agree with him, I also will say as you say, and confess myself deceived. But if you cannot remember the thing, then surely I will write as I have done, and as mine own remembrance serveth me. For as I will take good heed that there be in my book nothing false, so if there be anything in doubt, I will rather tell a lie than make a lie; because I had rather be good than wily.

Howbeit this matter may easily be remedied, if you will take the pains to ask the question of Raphael himself by word of mouth, if he be now with you, or else by your letters. Which you must needs do for another doubt also that hath chanced, through whose fault I cannot tell: whether through mine, or yours, or Raphael's. For neither we remembered to inquire of him, nor he to telll us, in what part of that new world Utopia is situate. The which thing, I had rather have spent no small sum of money, than that it should thus have escaped us; as well for that I am ashamed to be ignorant in what sea that island standeth, whereof I write so long a treatise, as also because there be with us certain men, and especially one virtuous and godly man, and a professor of divinity, who is exceeding desirous to go unto Utopia; not for a vain and curious desire to see news, but to the intent he may further and increase our religion, which is there already luckily begun. And that he may the better accomplish and perform this his good intent, he is minded to procure that he may be sent thither by the high bishop; yea, and that he himself may be made bishop of Utopia, being nothing scrupulous herein, that he must obtain this bishopric with suit. For he counteth that a godly suit which proceedeth not of the desire of honour or lucre, but only of a godly zeal.

Wherefore I most earnestly desire you, friend Peter, to talk with Hythloday, if you can, face to face, or else to write your letters to him, and so to work in this matter that in this my book there may neither anything be found which is untrue, neither anything be lacking which is true. And I think verily it shall be well done that you show unto him the book itself. For if I have missed or failed in any point, or if any fault have escaped me, no man can so well correct and amend it as he can; and yet that can he not do, unless he peruse and read over my book written. Moreover by this means shall you perceive whether he be well willing and content that I should undertake to put this work in writing. For if he be minded to publish and put forth his own labours and travels himself, perchance he would be loath, and so would I also, that in publishing the Utopian weal public, I should prevent him, and take from him the flower and grace of the novelty of this his history.

Howbeit, to say the very truth, I am not yet fully determined with myself whether I will put forth my book or no. For the natures of men be so divers, the fantasies of some so wayward, their minds so unkind, their judgments so corrupt, that they which lead a merry and a jocund life, following their own sensual pleasures and carnal lusts, may seem to be in a much better state or case than they that vex and unquiet themselves with cares and study for the putting forth and publishing of some thing that may be either profit or pleasure to others; which others nevertheless will disdainfully, scornfully, and unkindly accept the same. The most part of all be unlearned, and a great number hath learning in contempt. The rude and barbarous alloweth nothing but that which is very barbarous indeed. If it be one that hath a little smack of learning, he rejecteth as homely gear and common ware whatsoever is not stuffed full of old moth-eaten terms, and that be worn out of use. Some there be that have pleasure only in old rusty antiquities, and some only in their own doings. One is so sour, so crabbed, and so unpleasant, that he can away with no mirth nor sport. Another is so narrow between the shoulders, that he can bear no jests nor taunts. Some silly poor souls be so afraid that at every snappish word their nose shall be bitten off, that they stand in no less dread of every quick and sharp word than he that is bitten of a mad dog feareth water. Some be so mutable and wavering, that every hour they be in a new mind, saying one thing sitting and another thing standing. Another sort sitteth upon their ale-benches, and there among their cups they give judgment of the wits of writers, and with great authority they condemn even as pleaseth them every writer according to his writing, in most spiteful manner mocking, louting, and flouting them, being themselves in the mean season safe, and as sayeth the proverb, out of all danger of gunshot. For why, they be so smug and smooth, that they have not so much as one hair of an honest man whereby one may take hold of them. There be, moreover, some so unkind and ungentle, that though they take great pleasure and delectation in the work, yet for all that they cannot find in their hearts to love the author thereof, nor to afford him a good word, being much like uncourteous, unthankful, and churlish guests, which when they have with good and dainty meats well filled their bellies, depart home, giving no thanks to the feast-maker. Go your ways now, and make a costly feast at your own charges for guests so dainty-mouthed, so diverse in taste, and besides that of so unkind and unthankful natures.

But nevertheless, friend Peter, do, I pray you, with Hythloday as I willed you before. And as for this matter I shall be at my liberty afterwards to take new advisement. Howbeit, seeing I have taken great pains and labour in writing the matter, if it may stand with his mind and pleasure, I will, as touching the edition or publishing of the book, follow the counsel and advice of my friends, and specially yours. Thus fare you well, right heartily beloved friend Peter, with your gentle wife; and love me as you have ever done, for I love you better than ever I did.

TO THE RIGHT HONOURABLE

Jerome Busleyden,

PROVOST OF AIRE, AND COUNSELLOR
TO THE CATHOLIC KING CHARLES,
PETER GILES,CITIZEN OF ANTWERP,
WISHETH HEALTH AND FELICITY

Thomas More, the singular ornament of this our age, as you yourself (right honourable Busleyden) can witness, to whom he is perfectly well known, sent unto me this other day the island of Utopia, to very few as yet known, but most worthy, which as far excelling Plato's commonwealth, all people should be willing to know; specially of a man most eloquent, so finely set forth, so cunningly painted out, and so evidently subject to the eye, that as oft as I read it, methinketh that I see somewhat more than when I heard Raphael Hythloday himself (for I was present at that talk as well as Master More) uttering and pronouncing his own words: yea, though the same man, according to his pure eloquence, did so open and declare the matter, that he might plainly enough appear to report not things which he had learned of others only by hearsay, but which he had with his own eyes presently seen, and thoroughly viewed, and wherein he had no small time been conversant and abiding; a man truly, in mine opinion, as touching the knowledge of regions, peoples, and worldly experience, much passing, yea, even the very famous and renowned traveller Ulysses; and indeed such a one as for the space of these eight hundred years past I think nature into the world brought not forth his like; in comparison of whom Vespucci may be thought to have seen nothing. Moreover, whereas we be wont more effectually and pithily to declare and express things that we have seen, than which we have but only heard, there was besides that in this man a certain peculiar grace, and singular dexterity to describe and set forth a matter withal.

Yet the selfsame things as oft as I behold and consider them drawn and painted out with Master More's pencil, I am therewith so moved, so delighted, so inflamed, and so rapt, that sometimes methink I am presently conversant even in the island of Utopia. And I promise you, I can scant believe that Raphael himself by all that five years' space that he was in Utopia abiding, saw there so much as here in Master More's description is to be seen and perceived. Which description with so many wonders and miraculous things is replenished, that I stand in great doubt whereat first and chiefly to muse or marvel; whether at the excellency of his perfect and sure memory, which could wellnigh word by word rehearse so many things once only heard; or else at his singular prudence, who so well and wittily marked and bore away all the original causes and fountains (to the vulgar people commonly most unknown) whereof both issueth and springeth the mortal confusion and utter decay of a commonwealth, and also the advancement and wealthy state of the same may rise and grow; or else at the efficacy and pith of his words, which in so fine a Latin style, with such force of eloquence hath couched together and comprised so many and divers matters, specially being a man continually encumbered with so many busy and troublesome cares, both public and private, as he is.

Howbeit all these things cause you little to marvel (right honourable Busleyden), for that you are familiarly and thoroughly acquainted with the notable, yea almost divine wit of the man.

But now to proceed to other matters, I surely know nothing needful or requisite to be adjoined unto his writings. Only a metre of four verses written in the Utopian tongue, which after Master More's departure Hythloday by chance showed me, that have I caused to be added thereto, with the alphabet of the same nation. For, as touching the situation of the island, that is to say, in what part of the world Utopia standeth, the ignorance and lack whereof not a little troubleth and grieveth Master More, indeed Raphael left not that unspoken of. Howbeit with very few words he lightly touched it, incidentally by the way passing it over, as meaning of likelihood to keep and reserve that to another place. And the same, I wot not how, by a certain evil and unlucky chance escaped us both. For when Raphael was speaking thereof, one of Master More's servants came to him and whispered in his ear. Wherefore, I being then of purpose more earnestly addicted to hear, one of the company, by reason of cold taken, I think, a shipboard, coughed out so loud, that he took from my hearing certain of his words. But I will never stint, nor rest, until I have got the full and exact knowledge hereof; insomuch that I will be able perfectly to instruct you, not only in the longitude or true meridian of the island, but also in the just latitude thereof, that is to say, in the sublevation or height of the pole in that region, if our friend Hythloday be in safety, and alive.

For we hear very uncertain news of him. Some report that he died in his journey homeward. Some again affirm that he returned into his country, but partly for that he could not away with the fashions of his country folk, and partly for that his mind and affection was altogether set and fixed upon Utopia, they say that he hath taken his voyage thitherward again.

Now as touching this, that the name of this island is nowhere found among the old and ancient cosmographers, this doubt Hythloday himself very well dissolved. 'For why it is possible enough,' (quoth he) 'that the name, which it had in old time, was afterward changed, or else that they never had knowledge of this island: forasmuch as now in our time divers lands be found, which to the old geographers were unknown.' Howbeit, what needeth it in this behalf to fortify the matter with arguments, seeing Master More is author hereof sufficient?

But whereas he doubteth of the edition or imprinting of the book, indeed herein I both commend, and also acknowledge the man's modesty. Howbeit unto me it seemeth a work most unworthy to be long suppressed, and most worthy to go abroad into the hands of men, yea, and under the title of your name to be published to the world, either because the singular endowments and qualities of Master More be to no man better known than to you, or else because no man is more fit and meet than you with good counsels to further and advance the commonwealth, wherein you have many years already continued and travailed with great glory and commendation, both of wisdom and knowledge, and also of integrity and uprightness. Thus, O liberal supporter of good learning, and flower of this our time, I bid you most heartily well to fare. At Antwerp, 1516, the first day of November.

Thomas More sends his Best Wishes
to his own Peter Giles

I have been highly delighted, my dearest Peter, with the criticism, which has come also to your ears, of that very clever man who in regard to my *Utopia* employs the following dilemma. 'If it is supposed to be true, I consider some details to be rather absurd; if fictitious, I should like to know More's real opinion about some of the matters he relates.'

Whoever this man may be, Peter (and I suspect him to be learned and feel sure he is a friend), I am most grateful to him. Indeed I do not know that anyone, since the book was published, has given me such pleasure as he has by his candid criticism. First of all it is gratifying to find that, whether out of friendship to me or out of real interest in the book, he has not wearied of the task of reading it to the very end. Nor has he read it cursorily or hastily, as priests read their breviaries, those, that is to say, who read them at all, but so slowly and carefully that he weighs carefully every point as he proceeds. Then by the very fact that he disagrees with certain points, he makes it sufficiently evident that his agreement with the rest is not rash but considered. Lastly, by the very terms which he employs to blame me, he confers on me, indirectly, much more praise than have those who have tried to flatter me. For a man who, on reading something faulty that I may have written, complains that he has been disappointed, clearly shows what a high opinion he has conceived of me. As for myself, on the other hand, if out of all that I have written some few details at least should not be entirely absurd, it is much more than I ventured to hope for.

But (for I want, in my turn, to be equally open with him) I do not see why he should pride himself on being so sharp-sighted (or, as the Greeks call it, ὀξυδερχής) as to find some of the Utopian customs rather absurd, or to consider that I have unwisely contrived certain features in my commonwealth, as if nowhere else in the world were there any absurdity, or as if out of all the philosophers no one, in laying down regulations for the state, the ruler, or the private house, had ever suggested anything that could be improved upon. As to which, if I were not restrained by the reverence I bear to the memory, consecrated by age, of great men, I could from any one of them extract propositions which everyone would surely agree with me in condemning.

But now as he doubts whether *Utopia* is real or imaginary, I in turn demand his real opinion. I do not indeed deny that if I had determined to write about a commonwealth, and the idea of one had formed itself in my mind, I would not perhaps have thought it a sin to add fictitious details so that the truth, thus coated with honey, might be more palatable to my readers. But in that case even if I had wished to abuse the ignorance of the unlearned, I should certainly not have omitted to insert indications by which scholars would easily have been able to see through my design. If I had done nothing else I should at least have given such names to the prince, the river, the city, the island, as would have warned the skilful reader that the island exists nowhere, that the city is of shadows, the river without water, and the prince without people. It would not have been difficult to do and would have been much more witty. Unless truth had compelled me, I should certainly not have been so stupid as to use those outlandish, meaningless names, Utopia, Anyder, Amaurote, Ademus.

But, dear Giles, some men are so cautious. Whereas we, in simple faith, wrote out all that Hythloday narrated, they are so wary, so hard to satisfy, that they can scarcely be persuaded to believe it. At any rate, whatever they may think of the story, I am glad to think that they cannot call into question my own veracity, for I can say of my offspring what Mysis in Terence says to prove that the son of Glycery was not supposititious, 'Thank God there were reputable witnesses present at the birth.' For it has, indeed, turned out most fortunately for me that Raphael not only said what he did to you and to me, but to many other men of dignity and credit he said at least as much if not indeed more. Or if they are so unbelieving as not to trust even these, let them go to Hythloday himself, for he is yet living. Only recently I heard from some who had just come from Portugal that on March 1 last he was as well and strong as ever. Let them ask him, let them worm out the truth from him, if they please, by their questions, but let them understand that all I can do is to reproduce the story faithfully, not to guarantee the truth of what I was told.

Farewell, my dearest Peter, with your delightful wife and clever daughter, to whom my wife sends her best wishes.

THE FIRST BOOK
OF THE COMMUNICATION OF
RAPHAEL HYTHLODAY,
CONCERNING THE BEST STATE
OF A COMMONWEALTH

Concerning the Best State of a Commonwealth

The most victorious and triumphant King of England, Henry, the Eighth of that name, in all royal virtues a Prince most peerless, had of late in controversy with Charles, the right high and mighty King of Castile, weighty matters and of great importance. For the debatement and final determination whereof, the King's Majesty sent me ambassador into Flanders, joined in Commission with Cuthbert Tunstall, a man doubtless out of comparison, and whom the King's Majesty of late, to the great rejoicing of all men, did prefer to the office of Master of the Rolls.

But of this man's praises I will say nothing, not because I do fear that small credence shall be given to the testimony that cometh out of a friend's mouth; but because his virtue and learning be greater, and of more excellency, than that I am able to praise them, and also in all places so famous and so perfectly well known, that they need not, nor ought not of me to be praised, unless I would seem to show and set forth the brightness of the sun with a candle, as the proverb sayeth.

There met us at Bruges (for thus it was before agreed) they whom their Prince had for that matter appointed Commissioners, excellent men all. The chief and the head of them was the Margrave (as they call him) of Bruges, a right honourable man; but the wisest and the best spoken of them was George Temsice, provost of Cassel, a man not only by learning, but also by nature, of singular eloquence, and in the laws profoundly learned; but in reasoning and debating of matters, what by his natural wit, and what by daily exercise, surely he had few fellows. After that we had once or twice met, and upon certain points or articles could not fully and thoroughly agree, they for a certain space took their leave of us, and departed to Brussels, there to know their Prince's pleasure. I in the meantime (for so my business lay) went straight thence to Antwerp.

Whilst I was there abiding, oftentimes among others, but which to
me was more welcome than any other, did visit me one Peter Giles, a
citizen of Antwerp, a man there in his country of honest reputation,
and also preferred to high promotions, worthy truly of the highest.
For it is hard to say whether the young man be in learning or in
honesty more excellent. For he is both of wonderful virtuous
conditions, and also singularly well learned, and towards all sorts of
people exceeding gentle, but towards his friends so kind-hearted, so
loving, so faithful, so trusty, and of so earnest affection, that it were
very hard in any place to find a man that with him in all points of
friendship may be compared. No man can be more lowly or
courteous. No man useth less simulation or dissimulation; in no man
is more prudent simplicity. Besides this, he is in his talk and
communication so merry and pleasant, yea and that without harm,
that through his gentle entertainment, and his sweet and delectable
communication, in me was greatly abated and diminished the fervent
desire that I had to see my native country, my wife and my children,
whom then I did much long and covet to see, because that at that
time I had been more than four months from them.

Upon a certain day when I had heard the divine service in Our
Lady's Church, which is the fairest, the most gorgeous and curious
church of building in all the City, and also most frequented of people,
and the service being done, was ready to go home to my lodging, I
chanced to espy this foresaid Peter talking with a certain stranger, a
man well stricken in age, with a black, sunburnt face, a long beard,
and a cloak cast homely about his shoulders, whom, by his favour and
apparel, forthwith I judged to be a mariner. But the said Peter seeing
me, came unto me and saluted me. And as I was about to answer
him: 'See you this man?' sayeth he (and therewith he pointed to the
man that I saw him talking with before). 'I was minded,' quoth he,
'to bring him straight home to you.'

'He should have been very welcome to me,' said I, 'for your sake.'

'Nay' (quoth he), 'for his own sake, if you knew him; for there is
no man this day living that can tell you of so many strange and
unknown peoples and countries as this man can. And I know well
that you be very desirous to hear of such news.'

'Then I conjectured not far amiss' (quoth I), 'for even at the first
sight I judged him to be a mariner.'

'Nay' (quoth he), 'there ye were greatly deceived: he hath sailed, indeed, not as the mariner Palinurus, but as the expert and prudent prince Ulysses: yea, rather as the ancient and sage philosopher Plato. For this same Raphael Hythloday (for this is his name) is very well learned in the Latin tongue; but profound and excellent in the Greek language. Wherein he ever bestowed more study than in the Latin, because he had given himself wholly to the study of philosophy. Whereof he knew that there is nothing extant in Latin that is to any purpose, saving a few of Seneca's and Cicero's doings. His patrimony that he was born unto, he left to his brethren (for he is a Portugal born), and for the desire that he had to see and know the far countries of the world, he joined himself in company with Amerigo Vespucci, and in the three last voyages of those four that be now in print and abroad in every man's hands, he continued still in his company, saving that in the last voyage he came not home again with him. For he made such means and shift, what by intreatance, and what by importune suit, that he got licence of Master Amerigo (though it were sore against his will) to be one of the twenty-four which in the end of the last voyage were left in the country of Gulike. He was therefore left behind for his mind's sake, as one that took more thought and care for travelling than dying: having customably in his mouth these sayings: he that hath no grave, is covered with the sky: and, the way to heaven out of all places is of like length and distance. Which fantasy of his (if God had not been his better friend) he had surely bought full dear.

'But after the departing of Master Vespucci, when he had travelled through and about many countries with five of his companions, Gulikianes, at the last by marvellous chance he arrived in Taprobane, from whence he went to Calicut, where he chanced to find certain of his country's ships, wherein he returned again into his country, nothing less than looked for.'

All this when Peter had told me, I thanked him for his gentle kindness, that he had vouchsafed to bring me to the speech of that man, whose communication he thought should be to me pleasant and acceptable. And therewith I turned me to Raphael. And when we had hailed each other, and had spoken these common words that be customably spoken at the first meeting and acquaintance of strangers, we went thence to my house, and there in my garden, upon a bench covered with green turf, we sat down talking together.

There he told us how that, after the departing of Vespucci, he and his fellows that tarried behind in Gulike began by little and little, through fair and gentle speech, to win the love and favour of the people of that country, insomuch that within short space they did dwell amongst them, not only harmless, but also occupying with them very familiarly. He told us also that they were in high reputation and favour with a certain great man (whose name and country is now quite out of my remembrance), which of his mere liberality did bear the costs and charges of him and his five companions, and besides that gave them a trusty guide to conduct them in their journey (which by water was in boats, and by land in wagons) and to bring them to other Princes with very friendly commendations. Thus after many days' journeys, he said, they found towns, and cities, and weal publics, full of people, governed by good and wholesome laws.

For under the line equinoctial, and on both sides of the same, as far as the sun doth extend his course, lieth (quoth he) great and wide deserts and wildernesses, parched, burned, and dried up with continual and intolerable heat. All things be hideous, terrible, loathsome, and unpleasant to behold; all things out of fashion and comeliness, inhabited with wild beasts and serpents, or, at the leastwise, with people that be no less savage, wild, and noisome than the very beasts themselves be. But a little farther beyond that, all things begin by little and little to wax pleasant; the air soft, temperate, and gentle; the ground covered with green grass; less wildness in the beasts. At the last shall ye come again to people, cities, and towns wherein is continual intercourse and occupying of merchandise and chaffer, not only among themselves and with their borderers, but also with merchants of far countries, both by land and water.

'There I had occasion' (said he) 'to go to many countries on every side. For there was no ship ready to any voyage or journey, but I and my fellows were into it very gladly received.'

The ships that they found first were made plain, flat and broad in the bottom, troughwise. The sails were made of great rushes, or of wickers, and in some places of leather. Afterward they found ships with ridged keels, and sails of canvas, yea, and shortly after, having all things like ours; the shipmen also very expert and cunning, both in the sea and in the weather. But he said that he found great favour and friendship among them for teaching them the feat and the use of the loadstone, which to them before that time was unknown; and therefore they were wont to be very timorous and fearful upon the sea, nor to venture upon it, but only in the summer time. But now they have such a confidence in that stone that they fear not stormy winter; in so doing farther from care than danger. Insomuch that it is greatly to be doubted lest that thing, through their own foolish hardiness, shall turn them to evil and harm, which at the first was supposed should be to them good and commodious.

But what he told us that he saw in every country where he came, it were very long to declare. Neither is it my purpose at this time to make rehearsal thereof. But peradventure in another place I will speak of it, chiefly such things as shall be profitable to be known, as in special be those decrees and ordinances that he marked to be well and wittily provided and enacted among such peoples as do live together in a civil policy and good order. For of such things did we busily inquire and demand of him, and he likewise very willingly told us of the same. But as for monsters, because they be no news, of them we were nothing inquisitive. For nothing is more easy to be found than be barking Scyllas, ravening Celenos, and Lestrygones, devourers of people, and suchlike great and incredible monsters. But to find citizens ruled by good and wholesome laws, that is an exceeding rare and hard thing.

But as he marked many fond and foolish laws in those new-found lands, so he rehearsed divers acts and constitutions, whereby these our cities, nations, countries, and kingdoms may take example to amend their faults, enormities, and errors. Whereof in another place (as I said) I will intreat. Now at this time I am determined to rehearse only that he told us of the manners, customs, laws, and ordinances of the Utopians. But first I will repeat our former communication by the occasion, and (as I might say) the drift whereof he was brought into the mention of that weal public.

For, when Raphael had very prudently touched divers things that be amiss, some here and some there, yea, very many on both parts, and again had spoken of such wise laws and prudent decrees as be established and used, both here among us and also there among them, as a man so perfect and expert in the laws and customs of every several country, as though into what place soever he came guestwise, there he had led all his life: then Peter much marvelling at the man, 'Surely, Master Raphael' (quoth he), 'I wonder greatly why you get you not into some king's court. For I am sure there is no prince living that would not be very glad of you, as a man not only able highly to delight him with your profound learning, and this your knowledge of countries and peoples, but also meet to instruct him with examples,

and help him with counsel. And thus doing, you shall bring yourself
in a very good case, and also be of ability to help all your friends and
kinsfolk.'

'As concerning my friends and kinsfolk' (quoth he) 'I pass not greatly
for them, for I think I have sufficiently done my part towards them
already. For these things that other men do not depart from until they
be old and sick, yea, which they be then very loath to leave, when
they can no longer keep, those very same things did I, being not only
lusty and in good health, but also in the flower of my youth, divide
among my friends and kinsfolk; which I think with this my liberality
ought to hold them contented, and not to require nor to look that,
besides this, I should for their sakes give myself in bondage unto kings.'

'Nay, God forbid that' (quoth Peter). 'It is not my mind that you
should be in bondage to kings, but as a retainer to them at your
pleasure, which surely I think is the nighest way that you can devise
how to bestow your time fruitfully, not only for the private
commodity of your friends, and for the general profit of all sorts of
people, but also for the advancement of yourself to a much wealthier
state and condition than you be now in.'

'To a wealthier condition' (quoth Raphael) 'by that means that my
mind standeth clean against? Now I live at liberty after mine own
mind and pleasure, which I think very few of these great states and
peers of realms can say. Yea, and there be enough of them that sue for
great men's friendships: and therefore think it no great hurt if they
have not me, nor three or four such other as I am.'

'Well, I perceive plainly, friend Raphael' (quoth I), 'that you be
desirous neither of riches nor of power. And truly I have in no less
reverence and estimation a man of your mind, than any of them all
that be so high in power and authority. But you shall do as it
becometh you, yea, and according to this wisdom, to this high and
free courage of yours, if you can find in your heart so to appoint and
dispose yourself, that you may apply your wit and diligence to the
profit of the weal public, though it be somewhat to your own pain
and hindrance. And this shall you never so well do, nor with so great
profit perform, as if you be of some great prince's council, and put
into his head (as I doubt not but you will) honest opinions and
virtuous persuasions. For from the prince, as from a perpetual well-
spring, cometh among the people the flood of all that is good or evil.
But in you is so perfect learning, that without any experience, and

again so great experience, that without any learning, you may well be any king's counsellor.'

'You be twice deceived, Master More' (quoth he), 'first in me, and again in the thing itself. For neither is in me the ability that you force upon me, and if it were never so much, yet in disquieting mine own quietness I should nothing further the weal public. For first of all, the most part of all princes have more delight in warlike matters and feats of chivalry (the knowledge whereof I neither have nor desire) than in the good feats of peace; and employ much more study, how by right or by wrong to enlarge their dominions, than how well and peaceably to rule and govern what they have already. Moreover, they that be counsellors to kings, every one of them either is of himself so wise indeed that he needeth not, or else he thinketh himself so wise that he will not allow, another man's counsel, saving that they do shamefully and flatteringly give assent to the fond and foolish sayings of certain great men. Whose favours, because they be in high authority with their prince, by assentation and flattery they labour to obtain. And verily it is naturally given to all men to esteem their own inventions best. So both the raven and the ape think their own young ones fairest.

'Then if a man in such a company, where some disdain and have despite at other men's inventions, and some count their own best, if among such men (I say) a man should bring forth anything that he hath read done in times past, or that he hath seen done in other places, there the hearers fare as though the whole existimation of their wisdom were in jeopardy to be overthrown and that ever after they should be counted for very dizzards, unless they could in other men's inventions pick out matter to reprehend and find fault at. If all other poor helps fail, then this is their extreme refuge. "These things" (say they) "pleased our forefathers and ancestors; would God we could be so wise as they were": and as though they had wittily concluded the matter, and with this answer stopped every man's mouth, they sit down again. As who should say, it were a very dangerous matter if a man in any point should be found wiser than his forefathers were. And yet be we content to suffer the best and wittiest of their decrees to lie unexecuted: but if in anything a better order might have been taken than by them was, there we take fast hold, finding therein many faults. Many times have I chanced upon such proud, lewd, overthwart, and wayward judgments, yea, and once in England.'

'I pray you, sir' (quoth I), 'have you been in our country?'

'Yea, forsooth' (quoth he), 'and there I tarried for the space of four or five months together, not long after the insurrection that the western Englishmen made against their king, which by their own miserable and pitiful slaughter was suppressed and ended.

'In the mean season I was much bound and beholden to the right reverend father, John Morton, Archbishop and Cardinal of Canterbury, and at that time also Lord Chancellor of England; a man, Master Peter (for Master More knoweth already that I will say), not more honourable for his authority than for his prudence and virtue. He was of a mean stature, and though stricken in age, yet bore he his body upright. In his face did shine such an amiable reverence as was pleasant to behold, gentle in communication, yet earnest and sage. He had great delight many times with rough speech to his suitors, to prove, but without harm, what prompt wit and what bold spirit were in every man. In the which, as in a virtue much agreeing with his nature, so that therewith were not joined impudence, he took great delectation. And the same person, as apt and meet to have an administration in the weal public, he did lovingly embrace. In his speech he was fine, eloquent, and pithy. In the law he had profound knowledge, in wit he was incomparable, and in memory wonderful excellent. These qualities, which in him were by nature singular, he by learning and use had made perfect.

'The King put much trust in his counsel, the weal public also in a manner leaned unto him, when I was there. For even in the chief of his youth he was taken from school into the court, and there passed all his time in much trouble and business, being continually tumbled and tossed in the waves of divers misfortunes and adversities. And so by many and great dangers he learned the experience of the world, which so being learned cannot easily be forgotten.

'It chanced on a certain day, when I sat at his table, there was also a certain layman cunning in the laws of your realm. Who, I cannot tell whereof taking occasion, began diligently and earnestly to praise that strait and rigorous justice which at that time was there executed upon felons, who, as he said, were for the most part twenty hanged together upon one gallows. And, seeing so few escaped punishment, he said he could not choose but greatly wonder and marvel, how and by what evil luck it should so come to pass, that thieves nevertheless were in every place so rife and so rank.

' "Nay, sir," quoth I (for I durst boldly speak my mind before the

Cardinal), "marvel nothing hereat; for this punishment of thieves passeth the limits of justice, and is also very hurtful to the weal public. For it is too extreme and cruel a punishment for theft, and yet not sufficient to refrain and withhold men from theft. For simple theft is not so great an offence that it ought to be punished with death. Neither there is any punishment so horrible that it can keep them from stealing which have no other craft whereby to get their living. Therefore in this point, not you only, but also the most part of the world, be like evil schoolmasters, which be readier to beat, than to teach, their scholars. For great and horrible punishments be appointed for thieves, whereas much rather provision should have been made that there were some means whereby they might get their living, so that no man should be driven to this extreme necessity, first to steal, and then to die."

' "Yes" (quoth he), "this matter is well enough provided for already. There be handicrafts, there is husbandry to get their living by, if they would not willingly be naught."

' "Nay" (quoth I), "you shall not escape so: for first of all, I will speak nothing of them that come home out of the wars maimed and lame, as not long ago out of Blackheath field, and a little before that out of the wars in France: such, I say, as put their lives in jeopardy for the weal public's or the king's sake, and by reason of weakness and lameness be not able to occupy their old crafts, and be too aged to learn new: of them I will speak nothing, forasmuch as wars have their ordinary recourses. But let us consider those things that chance daily before our eyes.

' "First there is a great number of gentlemen which cannot be content to live idle themselves, like drones, off that which others have laboured for: their tenants, I mean, whom they poll and shave to the quick, by raising their rents (for this only point of frugality do they use, men else through their lavish and prodigal spending able to bring themselves to very beggary), these gentlemen, I say, do not only live in idleness themselves, but also carry about with them at their tails a great flock or train of idle and loitering serving-men, which never learned any craft whereby to get their livings. These men, as soon as their master is dead, or be sick themselves, be incontinent thrust out of doors. For gentlemen had rather keep idle persons than sick men, and many times the dead man's heir is not able to maintain so great a house, and keep so many serving-men as his father did.

' "Then in the mean season, they that be thus destitute of service either starve for hunger, or manfully play the thieves. For what would you have them to do? When they have wandered abroad so long, until they have worn threadbare their apparel, and also impaired their health, then gentlemen, because of their pale and sickly faces and patched coats, will not take them into service. And husbandmen dare not set them a work; knowing well enough that he is nothing meet to do true and faithful service to a poor man with a spade and a mattock for small wages and hard fare, which being daintily and tenderly pampered up in idleness and pleasure, was wont with a sword and a buckler by his side to jet through the street with a bragging look, and to think himself too good to be any man's mate."

' "Nay by St Mary, sir" (quoth the lawyer), "not so. For this kind of men must we make most of. For in them as men of stouter stomachs, bolder spirits, and manlier courage than handicraftsmen and ploughmen be, doth consist the whole power, strength, and puissance of our army, when we must fight in battle."

' "Forsooth, sir, as well you might say" (quoth I) "that for war's sake you must cherish thieves. For surely you shall never lack thieves, while you have them. No, nor thieves be not the most false and faint-hearted soldiers, nor soldiers be not the cowardliest thieves: so well these two crafts agree together. But this fault, though it be much used among you, yet is it not peculiar to you only, but common also almost to all nations. Yet France besides this is troubled and infected with a much sorer plague. The whole realm is filled and besieged with hired soldiers in peace time (if that be peace) which be brought in under the same colour and pretence that hath persuaded you to keep these idle serving-men. For these wise fools and very archdolts thought the wealth of the whole country herein to consist, if there were ever in a readiness a strong and a sure garrison, specially of old practised soldiers, for they put no trust at all in men unexercised. And therefore they must be forced to seek for war, to the end they may ever have practised soldiers and cunning manslayers, lest that (as it is prettily said of Sallust) their hands and their minds through idleness or lack of exercise should wax dull.

' "But how pernicious and pestilent a thing it is to maintain such beasts, the Frenchmen by their own harms have learned, and the examples of the Romans, Carthaginians, Syrians, and of many other countries do manifestly declare. For not only the Empire, but also the fields and cities of all these, by divers occasions have been overrun and destroyed of their own armies beforehand had in a readiness. Now how unnecessary a thing this is, hereby it may appear: that the French soldiers, which from their youth have been practised and inured in feats of arms, do not crack nor advance themselves to have very often got the upper hand and mastery of your new-made and unpractised soldiers. But in this point I will not use many words, lest perchance I may seem to flatter you. No, nor those same handicraftsmen of yours in cities, nor yet the rude and uplandish ploughmen of the country, are not supposed to be greatly afraid of your gentlemen's idle serving-men, unless it be such as be not of body or stature correspondent to their strength and courage, or else whose bold stomachs be discouraged through poverty. Thus you may see that it is not to be feared lest they should be effeminated, if they were brought up in good crafts and laboursome works, whereby to get their livings, whose stout and sturdy bodies (for gentlemen vouchsafe to corrupt and spill none but picked and chosen men) now either by reason of rest and idleness be brought to weakness; or else by too easy and womanly exercises be made feeble and unable to endure hardness. Truly howsoever the case standeth, this methinketh is nothing available to the weal public, for war's sake, which you never have but when you will yourselves, to keep and maintain an innumerable flock of that sort of men that be so troublesome and noyous in peace, whereof you ought to have a thousand times more regard than of war.

' "But yet this is not only the necessary cause of stealing. There is another, which, as I suppose, is proper and peculiar to you Englishmen alone."

' "What is that?" quoth the Cardinal.

' "Forsooth, my lord" (quoth I), "your sheep that were wont to be so meek and tame, and so small eaters, now, as I hear say, be become so great devourers and so wild that they eat up and swallow down the very men themselves. They consume, destroy, and devour whole fields, houses, and cities. For look in what parts of the realm doth grow the finest, and therefore dearest wool, there noblemen and gentlemen, yea, and certain abbots, holy men, no doubt, not contenting themselves with the yearly revenues and profits that were wont to grow to their forefathers and predecessors of their lands, nor being content that they live in rest and pleasure nothing profiting, yea much annoying the weal public, leave no ground for tillage, they enclose all into pastures; they throw down houses; they pluck down towns, and leave nothing standing, but only the church to be made a sheephouse. And as though you lost no small quantity of ground by forests, chases, lands, and parks, those good holy men turn all dwelling-places and all glebeland into desolation and wilderness.

' "Therefore that one covetous and unsatiable cormorant and very plague of his native country may compass about and enclose many thousand acres of ground together within one pale or hedge, the husbandmen be thrust out of their own, or else either by covin and fraud, or by violent oppression they be put beside it, or by wrongs and injuries they be so wearied that they be compelled to sell all: by one means, therefore, or by other, either by hook or crook they must needs depart away, poor, silly, wretched souls, men, women, husbands, wives, fatherless children, widows, woeful mothers with their young babes, and their whole household, small in substance and much in number, as husbandry requireth many hands. Away they trudge, I say, out of their known and accustomed houses, finding no place to rest in. All their household stuff, which is very little worth, though it might well abide the sale; yet being suddenly thrust out, they be constrained to sell it for a thing of naught. And when they have wandered abroad till that be spent, what can they then else do but steal, and then justly pardy be hanged, or else go about a-begging. And yet then also they be cast in prison as vagabonds, because they go about and work not, whom no man will set a-work, though they never so willingly proffer themselves thereto. For one shepherd or herdman is enough to eat up that ground with cattle, to the occupying whereof about husbandry many hands were requisite. And this is also the cause why victuals be now in many places dearer.

' "Yea, besides this, the price of wool is so risen, that poor folks, which were wont to work it, and make cloth thereof, be now able to buy none at all. And by this means very many be forced to forsake work, and to give themselves to idleness. For after that so much ground was enclosed for pasture, an infinite multitude of sheep died of the rot, such vengeance God took of their inordinate and unsociable covetousness, sending among the sheep that pestiferous murrain, which much more justly should have fallen on the sheepmasters' own heads.

' "And though the number of sheep increase ever so fast, yet the price falleth not one mite, because there be so few sellers. For they be almost all come into a few rich men's hands, whom no need forceth to sell before they list, and they list not before they may sell as dear as they list. Now the same cause bringeth in like dearth of the other kinds of cattle, yea, and that so much the more, because that after farms plucked down, and husbandry decayed, there is no man that passeth for the breeding of young store. For these rich men bring not up the young ones of great cattle as they do lambs. But first they buy them abroad very cheap, and afterwards when they be fatted in their pastures, they sell them again exceeding dear. And therefore (as I suppose) the whole incommodity hereof is not yet felt. For yet they make dearth only in those places where they sell. But when they shall fetch them away from thence where they be bred faster than they can be brought up, then shall there also be felt great dearth, store beginning there to fail where the ware is bought.

' "Thus the unreasonable covetousness of a few hath turned that thing to the utter undoing of your island, in the which thing the chief felicity of your realm did consist. For this great dearth of victuals causeth men to keep as little houses, and as small hospitality as they possibly may, and to put away their servants: whether, I pray you, but a-begging, or else (which the gentle bloods and stout stomachs will sooner set their minds unto) a-stealing?

' "Now to amend the matter, to this wretched beggary and miserable poverty is joined great wantonness, importunate superflu- ity, and excessive riot. For not only gentlemen's servants, but also handicraftsmen, yea, and almost the ploughmen of the country, with all other sorts of people, use much strange and proud newfangledness in their apparel, and too much prodigal riot and sumptuous fare at their table. Now bawds, queans, whores, harlots, strumpets, brothel- houses, stews, and yet another stews, wine-taverns, ale-houses, and tippling-houses, with so many naughty, lewd, and unlawful games, as dice, cards, tables, tennis, bowls, quoits, do not all these send the haunters of them straight a-stealing when their money is gone?

' "Cast out these pernicious abominations, make a law that they which plucked down farms and towns of husbandry shall re-edify them, or else yield and uprender the possession thereof to such as will go to the cost of building them anew. Suffer not these rich men to buy up all, to engross, and forestall, and with their monopoly to keep the market alone as pleases them. Let not so many be brought up in idleness, let husbandry and tillage be restored, let cloth-working be renewed, that there may be honest labours for this idle sort to pass their time in profitably, which hitherto either poverty hath caused to be thieves, or else now be either vagabonds or idle serving-men, and shortly will be thieves. Doubtless unless you find a remedy for these enormities, you shall in vain advance yourself of executing justice upon felons. For this justice is more beautiful in appearance, and more flourishing to the show, than either just or profitable. For by suffering your youth wantonly and viciously to be brought up, and to be infected, even from their tender age, by little and little with vice, then a God's name to be punished when they commit the same faults after being come to man's state, which from their youth they were ever like to do; in this point, I pray you, what other thing do you, than make thieves, and then punish them?"

'Now as I was thus speaking the lawyer began to make himself ready to answer, and was determined with himself to use the common fashion and trade of disputers, which be more diligent in rehearsing than answering, as thinking the memory worthy of the chief praise. "Indeed, sir" (quoth he), "you have said well, being but a stranger, and one that might rather hear something of these matters than have any exact or perfect knowledge of the same, as I will incontinent by open proffer make manifest and plain. For, first I will rehearse in order all that you have said; then I will declare wherein you be deceived, through lack of knowledge in all our fashions, manners and customs; and last of all I will answer your arguments, and confute them every one. First, therefore, I will begin where I promised. Four things you seemed to me."

' "Hold your peace," quoth the Cardinal, "for it appeareth that you will make no short answer, which make such a beginning. Wherefore at this time you shall not take the pains to make your answer, but keep it to your next meeting, which I would be right glad that it might be even tomorrow next, unless either you or Master Raphael have any earnest let.

' "But now, Master Raphael, I would very gladly hear of you, why you think theft not worthy to be punished with death, or what other punishment you can devise more expedient to the weal public. For I am sure you are not of that mind, that you would have theft escape unpunished. For if now the extreme punishment of death cannot cause them to leave stealing, then if ruffians and robbers should be sure of their lives, what violence, what fear were able to hold their hands from robbing, which would take the mitigation of the punishment as a very provocation to the mischief?"

' "Surely, my lord" (quoth I), "I think it not right nor justice, that the loss of money should cause the loss of man's life. For mine opinion is, that all the goods in the world are not able to countervail man's life. But if they would thus say: that the breaking of justice, and the transgression of the laws is recompensed with this punishment, and not the loss of the money, then why may not this extreme and rigorous justice well be called plain injury? For so cruel governance, so strait rules, and unmerciful laws be not allowable, that if a small offence be committed, by and by the sword should be drawn; nor so stoical ordinances are to be borne withal, as to count all offences of such equality, that the killing of a man, or the taking of his money from him were both a matter, and the one no more heinous offence than the other; between the which two, if we have any respect to equity, no similitude or equality consisteth. God commandeth us that we shall not kill. And be we then so hasty to kill a man for taking a little money? And if any man would understand killing by this commandment of God to be forbidden after no larger wise than man's constitutions define killing to be lawful, then why may it not likewise by man's constitutions be determined after what sort whoredom, fornication, and perjury may be lawful? For whereas, by the permission of God, no man neither hath power to kill neither himself nor yet any other man: then if a law made by the consent of men, concerning slaughter of men, ought to be of such strength, force, and virtue, that they which contrary to the commandment of God have killed those whom this constitution of man commanded to be killed, be clean quite and exempt out of the bonds and danger of God's commandment; shall it not then by this reason follow, that the power of God's commandment shall extend no further than man's law doth define and permit? And so shall it come to pass that in like manner man's constitutions in all things shall determine how far the observation of all God's commandments shall extend. To be short, Moses' law, though it were ungentle and sharp, as a law that was given to bondmen, yea, and them very obstinate, stubborn, and stiff-necked, yet it punished theft by the purse, and not with death. And let us not think that God in the new law of clemency and mercy, under the which He ruleth us with fatherly gentleness as His dear children, hath given us greater scope and licence to the execution of cruelty, one upon another.

' "Now ye have heard the reasons whereby I am persuaded that this punishment is unlawful. Furthermore, I think there is nobody that knoweth not how unreasonable, yea, how pernicious a thing it is to the weal public, that a thief and a homicide or murderer, should suffer equal and like punishment. For the thief seeing that man that is condemned for theft in no less jeopardy, nor judged to no less punishment, than him that is convicted of manslaughter, through this cogitation only he is strongly and forcibly provoked, and in a manner constrained, to kill him whom else he would have but robbed. For the murder being once done, he is in less fear, and in more hope that the deed shall not be betrayed or known, seeing the party is now dead and rid out of the way, which only might have uttered and disclosed it. But if he chance to be taken and descried: yet he is in no more danger and jeopardy than if he had committed but single felony. Therefore whiles we go about with such cruelty to make thieves afraid, we provoke them to kill good men.

' "Now as touching this question, what punishment were more commodious and better; that truly in my judgment is easier to be found, than what punishment might be worse. For why should we doubt that to be a good and a profitable way for the punishment of offenders, which we know did in times past so long please the Romans, men in the administration of a weal public most expert, politic, and cunning? Such as among them were conceived of great and heinous trespasses, them they condemned into stone quarries, and into mines to dig metal, there to be kept in chains all the days of their life.

' "But as concerning this matter, I allow the ordinance of no nation so well as that which I saw, while I travelled abroad about the world, used in Persia among the people that commonly be called the Polylerites. Whose land is both large and ample, and also well and wittily governed; and the people in all conditions free and ruled by their own laws, saving that they pay a yearly tribute to the great King of Persia. But because they be far from the sea, compassed and enclosed almost round about with high mountains, and do content themselves with the fruits of their own land, which is of itself very fertile and fruitful: for this cause neither they go to other countries, nor other come to them. And according to the old custom of the land, they desire not to enlarge the bounds of their dominions; and those that they have, by reason of the high hills, be easily defended;

and the tribute which they pay to their chief lord and king setteth
them quit and free from warfare. Thus their life is commodious rather
than gallant, and may better be called happy or wealthy, than notable
or famous. For they be not known as much as by name, I suppose,
saving only to their next neighbours and borderers.

' "They that in this land be attainted and convict of felony, make
restitution of that which they stole, to the right owner, and not (as
they do in other lands) to the king; whom they think to have no
more right to the thief-stolen thing than the thief himself hath. But if
the thing be lost or made away, then the value of it is paid of the
goods of such offenders, which else remaineth all whole to their
wives and children. And they themselves be condemned to be
common labourers, and, unless the theft be very heinous, they be
neither locked in prison, nor fettered in gyves, but be untied and go
at large, labouring in the common works. They that refuse labour, or
go slowly and slackly to their work, be not only tied in chains, but
also pricked forward with stripes. But being diligent about their work
they live without check or rebuke. Every night they be called in by
name, and be locked in their chambers. Beside their daily labour,
their life is nothing hard or incommodious. Their fare is indifferent
good, borne at the charges of the weal public, because they be
common servants to the commonwealth.

' "But their charges in all places of the land is not borne alike. For
in some parts that which is bestowed upon them is gathered of alms.
And though that way be uncertain, yet the people be so full of mercy
and pity, that none is found more profitable or plentiful. In some
places certain lands be appointed hereunto; of the revenues whereof
they be maintained. And in some places every man giveth a certain
tribute for the same use and purpose. Again, in some parts of the land
these serving-men (for so be these damned persons called) do no
common work, but as every private man needeth labourers, so he
cometh into the market-place, and there hireth some of them for
meat and drink, and a certain limited wages by the day, somewhat
cheaper than he should hire a freeman. It is also lawful for them to
chastise the sloth of these serving-men with stripes.

' "By this means they never lack work, and besides the gaining of
their meat and drink every one of them bringeth daily something into
the common treasury. All and every one of them be apparelled in one
colour. Their heads be not polled or shaven, but rounded a little

above the ears. And the tip of the one ear is cut off. Every one of them may take meat and drink of their friends, and also a coat of their own colour; but to receive money is death, as well to the giver as to the receiver. And no less jeopardy it is for a freeman to receive money of a serving-man for any manner of cause, and likewise for serving-men to touch weapons.

' "The serving-men of every several shire be distinct and known from other by their several and distinct badges, which to cast away is death; as it is also to be seen out of the precinct of their own shire, or to talk with a serving-man of another shire. And it is no less danger to them for to intend to run away than to do it indeed. Yea, and to conceal such an enterprise, in a serving-man it is death, in a freeman servitude. Of the contrary part, to him that openeth and uttereth such counsels, be decreed large gifts: to a freeman a great sum of money, to a serving-man freedom, and to them both forgiveness and pardon of that they were of counsel in that pretence. So that it can never be so good for them to go forward in their evil purpose, as by repentance to turn back.

' "This is the law and order in this behalf, as I have shown you. Wherein what humanity is used, how far it is from cruelty, and how commodious it is, you do plainly perceive; forasmuch as the end of their wrath and punishment intendeth nothing else but the destruction of vices and saving of men; with so using and ordering them that they cannot choose but be good, and what harm soever they did before, in the residue of their life to make amends for the same.

' "Moreover, it is so little feared that they should turn again to their vicious conditions, that wayfaring men will for their safeguard choose them to their guides before any other, in every shire changing and taking new. For if they would commit robbery, they have nothing about them meet for that purpose. They may touch no weapons: money found about them should betray the robbery. They should be no sooner taken with the manner, but forthwith they should be punished. Neither they can have any hope at all to escape away by flying. For how should a man, that in no part of his apparel is like other men, fly privily and unknown, unless he would run away naked? Howbeit so also flying he should be descried by the rounding of his head, and his ear-mark. But it is a thing to be doubted, that they will lay their heads together and conspire against the weal public. No, no, I warrant you. For the serving-men of one shire alone could never hope to bring to pass such an enterprise without soliciting, enticing, and alluring the serving-men of many other shires to take their parts. Which thing is to them so impossible, that they may not as much as speak or talk together, or salute one another. No, it is not to be thought that they would make their own countrymen and companions of their counsel in such a matter, which they know well should be jeopardy to the counsellor thereof, and great commodity and goodness to the opener and detector of the same. Whereas, on the other part, there is none of them all hopeless or in despair to recover again his former estate of freedom by humble obedience, by patient suffering, and by giving good tokens and likelihood of himself, that he will ever after that live like a true and an honest man. For every year divers of them be restored to their freedom, through the commendation of their patience."

'When I had thus spoken, saying, moreover, that I could see no cause why this order might not be had in England with much more profit than the justice which the lawyer so highly praised: "Nay," quoth the lawyer, "this could never be so established in England but that it must needs bring the weal public into great jeopardy and hazard." And as he was thus saying, he shook his head and made a wry mouth, and so he held his peace. And all that were there present, with one assent agreed to his saying.

' "Well" (quoth the Cardinal) "yet it were hard to judge without a proof, whether this order would do well here or no. But when the sentence of death is given, if then the king should command execution to be deferred and spared, and would prove this order and fashion, taking away the privileges of all centuries, if then the proof should declare the thing to be good and profitable, then it were well done that it were established; else the condemned and reprieved persons may as well and as justly be put to death after this proof, as when they were first cast. Neither any jeopardy can in the mean space grow hereof. Yea, and methinketh that these vagabonds may very well be ordered after the same fashion, against whom we have hitherto made so many laws, and so little prevailed."

'When the Cardinal had thus said, then every man gave great praise to my sayings, which a little before they had disallowed. But most of all was esteemed that which was spoken of vagabonds, because it was the Cardinal's own addition.

'I cannot tell whether it were best to rehearse the communication that followed, for it was not very sad. But yet you shall hear it, for there was no evil in it, and partly it pertained to the matter beforesaid.

'There chanced to stand by a certain jesting parasite, or scoffer, which would seem to resemble and counterfeit the fool. But he did in such wise counterfeit, that he was almost the very same indeed that he laboured to represent; he so studied with words and sayings brought forth so out of time and place to make sport and move laughter, that he himself was oftener laughed at than his jests were. Yet the foolish fellow brought out now and then such indifferent and reasonable stuff, that he made the proverb true, which saith: He that shooteth oft, at the last shall hit the mark. So that when one of the company said that through my communication a good order was found for thieves, and that the Cardinal also had well provided for vagabonds, so that only remained some good provision to be made for them that through sickness and age were fallen into poverty, and were become so impotent and unwieldy that they were not able to work for their living: "Tush" (quoth he), "let me alone with them: you shall see me do well enough with them. For I had rather than any good, that this kind of people were driven somewhere out of my sight, they have so sore troubled me many times and oft, when they have with their lamentable tears begged money of me: and yet they could never to my mind so tune their song, that thereby they ever got of me one farthing. For ever more the one of these two chanced: either that I would not, or else that I could not, because I had it not. Therefore now they be waxed wise. For when they see me go by, because they will not lose their labour, they let me pass and say not one word to me. So they look for nothing of me, no, in good sooth, no more than if I were a priest or a monk. But I will make a law that all these beggars shall be distributed and bestowed into houses of religion. The men shall be made lay brethren, as they call them, and the women nuns." Hereat the Cardinal smiled, and allowed it in jest, yea and all the residue in good earnest.

'But a certain friar, graduate in divinity, took such pleasure and delight in this jest of priests and monks, that he also being else a man of grisly and stern gravity, began merrily and wantonly to jest and taunt. "Nay" (quoth he), "you shall not so be rid and dispatched of beggars, unless you make some provision also for us friars."

' "Why" (quoth the jester), "that is done already, for my lord himself set a very good order for you, when he decreed that vagabonds should be kept straight, and set to work: for you be the greatest and veriest vagabonds that be."

'This jest also, when they saw the Cardinal not disprove it, every man took it gladly, saving only the friar. For he (and that no marvel) being thus touched on the quick, and hit on the gall, so fretted, so fumed, and chafed at it, and was in such a rage, that he could not refrain himself from chiding, scolding, railing, and reviling. He called the fellow ribald, villain, javel, backbiter, slanderer, and the child of perdition, citing therewith terrible threatenings out of holy scripture.

'Then the jesting scoffer began to play the scoffer indeed, and verily he was good at that, for he could play a part in that play no man better. "Patient yourself, good Master Friar" (quoth he), "and be not angry, for scripture saith: In your patience you shall save your souls."

'Then the friar (for I will rehearse his own very words): "No, gallous wretch, I am not angry" (quoth he), "or at the leastwise, I do not sin: for the psalmist saith, Be you angry, and sin not."

'Then the Cardinal spoke gently to the friar, and desired him to quiet himself.

'"No, my lord" (quoth he), "I speak not but of a good zeal as I ought; for holy men had a good zeal. Wherefore it is said: The zeal of thy house hath eaten me. And it is sung in the church: The scorners of Helizeus, while he went up into the house of God, felt the zeal of the bald, as peradventure this scorning villain ribald shall feel."

'"You do it" (quoth the Cardinal) "perchance of a good mind and affection: but methinketh you should do, I cannot tell whether more holily, certainly more wisely, if you would not set your wit to a fool's wit, and with a fool take in hand a foolish contention."

'"No, forsooth, my lord" (quoth he), "I should not do more wisely. For Solomon the wise saith: Answer a fool according to his folly, like as I do now, and do show him the pit that he shall fall into, if he take not heed. For if many scorners of Helizeus, which was but one bald man, felt the zeal of the bald, how much more shall one scorner of many friars feel, among whom be many bald men? And we have also the Pope's bulls, whereby all that mock and scorn us be excommunicated, suspended, and accursed."

'The Cardinal, seeing that no end would be made, sent away the jester by a privy beck, and turned the communication to another matter. Shortly after, when he was risen from the table, he went to hear his suitors, and so dismissed us.

'Look, Master More, with how long and tedious a tale I have kept you, which surely I would have been ashamed to have done, but that you so earnestly desired me, and did after such a sort give ear unto it, as though you would not that any parcel of that communication should be left out. Which though I have done somewhat briefly, yet could I not choose but rehearse it, for the judgment of them which, when they had improved and disallowed my sayings, yet incontinent hearing the Cardinal allow them, did themselves also approve the same, so impudently flattering him, that they were nothing ashamed to admit, yea, almost in good earnest, his jester's foolish inventions, because that he himself by smiling at them did seem not to disprove them. So that hereby you may right well perceive how little the courtiers would regard and esteem me and my sayings.'

'I ensure you, Master Raphael,' quoth I, 'I took great delectation in hearing you: all things that you said were spoken so wittily and so pleasantly. And me thought myself to be in the meantime, not only at home in my country, but also, through the pleasant remembrance of the Cardinal, in whose house I was brought up of a child, to wax a child again. And, friend Raphael, though I did bear very great love towards you before, yet seeing you do so earnestly favour this man, you will not believe how much my love towards you is now increased.

'But yet, all this notwithstanding, I can by no means change my mind, but that I must needs believe that you, if you be disposed, and can find in your heart to follow some prince's court, shall with your good counsels greatly help and further the commonwealth. Wherefore there is nothing more appertaining to your duty, that is to say, to the duty of a good man. For whereas your Plato judgeth that weal publics shall by this means attain perfect felicity, either if philosophers be kings, or else if kings gave themselves to the study of philosophy, how far, I pray you, shall commonwealths then be from this felicity if philosophers will vouchsafe* to instruct kings with their good counsel?'

'They be not so unkind' (quoth he), 'but they would gladly do it, yea, many have done it already in books that they have put forth, if kings and princes would be willing and ready to follow good counsel. But Plato doubtless did well foresee, unless kings themselves would apply their minds to the study of philosophy, that else they would

---

* The original has a negative: 'will not vouchsafe' gives a clearer meaning.

never thoroughly allow the counsel of philosophers, being themselves
before even from their tender age infected and corrupt with perverse
and evil opinions. Which thing Plato himself proved true in King
Dionysius. If I should propose to any king wholesome decrees, doing
my endeavour to pluck out of his mind the pernicious original causes
of vice and naughtiness, think you not that I should forthwith either
be driven away, or else made a laughing-stock?

'Well, suppose I were with the French king, and there sitting in his
council, while in that most secret consultation, the king himself there
being present in his own person, they beat their brains, and search the
very bottoms of their wits, to discuss by what craft and means the king
may still keep Milan, and draw to him again fugitive Naples, and then
how to conquer the Venetians, and how to bring under his jurisdiction all Italy, then how to win the dominion of Flanders, Brabant, and
of all Burgundy, with divers other lands, whose kingdoms he hath
long ago in mind and purpose invaded. Here while one counselleth to
conclude a league of peace with the Venetians, so long to endure as
shall be thought meet and expedient for their purpose, and to make
them also of their council, yea, and besides that to give them part of
the prey, which afterward, when they have brought their purpose
about after their own minds, they may require and claim again.
Another thinketh best to hire the Germans. Another would have the
favour of the Swiss won with money. Another's advice is to appease
the puissant power of the Emperor's majesty with gold, as with a most
pleasant and acceptable sacrifice. While another giveth counsel to
make peace with the King of Aragon, and to restore unto him his own
kingdom of Navarre as a full assurance of peace. Another cometh in
with his five eggs, and adviseth to hook in the King of Castile with
some hope of affinity or alliance, and to bring to their part certain peers
of his court for great pensions. While they all stay at the chiefest doubt
of all, what to do in the meantime with England, and yet agree all in
this to make peace with the Englishmen, and with most sure and
strong bands to bind that weak and feeble friendship, so that they must
be called friends, and had in suspicion as enemies. And that therefore
the Scots must be had in readiness, as it were in a standing ready at all
occasions, in aunters the Englishmen should stir never so little,
incontinent to set upon them. And, moreover, privily and secretly (for
openly it may not be done by the truce that is taken), privily, thereof, I
say, to make much of some peer of England that is banished his

country, which must claim title to the crown of the realm, and affirm himself just inheritor thereof, that by this subtle means they may hold to them the king, in whom else they have but small trust and affiance.

'Here, I say, where so great and high matters be in consultation, where so many noble and wise men counsel their king only to war, here if I, silly man, should rise up and will them to turn over the leaf, and learn a new lesson, saying that my counsel is not to meddle with Italy, but to tarry still at home, and that the kingdom of France alone is almost greater than that it may well be governed of one man; so that the king should not need to study how to get more: and then should propose unto them the decrees of the people that be called the Achoriens, which be situate over against the Island of Utopia on the south-east side.

'These Achoriens once made war in their king's quarrel for to get him another kingdom which he laid claim unto, and advanced himself right inheritor to the crown thereof, by the title of an old alliance. At the last when they had got it, and saw that they had even as much vexation and trouble in keeping it as they had in getting it, and that either their new conquered subjects by sundry occasions were making daily insurrections to rebel against them, or else that other countries were continually with diverse inroads and foragings invading them; so that they were ever fighting either for them or against them, and never could break up their camps: seeing themselves in the mean season pilled and impoverished; their money carried out of the realm; their own men killed to maintain the glory of another nation; when they had no war, peace nothing better than war, by reason that their people in war had so inured themselves to corrupt and wicked manners; that they had taken a delight and pleasure in robbing and stealing; that through manslaughter they had gathered boldness to mischief; that their laws were had in contempt, and nothing set by or regarded; that their king being troubled with the charge and governance of two kingdoms, could not nor was not able perfectly to discharge his office towards them both; seeing again that all these evils and troubles were endless; at the last laid their heads together, and like faithful and loving subjects gave to their king free choice and liberty to keep still the one of these two kingdoms whether he would; alleging that he was not able to keep both, and that they were more than might well be governed of half a king; forasmuch as no man would be content to take him for his muleteer that keepeth another man's mules besides his. So this good prince was constrained to be content with his old kingdom, and to give over the new to one of his friends, who shortly after was violently driven out.

'Furthermore, if I should declare unto them that all this busy preparance for war, whereby so many nations for his sake should be brought into a troublesome hurly-burly, when all his coffers were emptied, his treasures wasted, and his people destroyed, should at the length through some mischance be in vain and to none effect; and that therefore it were best for him to content himself with his own kingdom of France, as his forefathers and predecessors did before him, to make much of it, to enrich it, and to make it as flourishing as he could, to endeavour himself to love his subjects, and again to be beloved of them, willingly to live with them, peaceably to govern them, and with other kingdoms not to meddle, seeing that which he hath already is even enough for him, yea and more than he can well turn him to; this mine advice, Master More, how think you it would be heard and taken?'

'So God help me not very thankfully,' quoth I.

'Well, let us proceed then,' quoth he. 'Suppose that some king and his council were together whetting their wits and devising what subtle craft they might invent to enrich the king with great treasures of money. First one counselleth to raise and enhance the valuation of money when the king must pay any; and again to call down the value of coin to less than it is worth when he must receive or gather any. For thus great sums shall be paid with a little money, and where little is due, much shall be received. Another counselleth to feign war, that when under this colour and pretence the king hath gathered great abundance of money, he may, when it shall please him, make peace with great solemnity and holy ceremonies, to blind the eyes of the poor commonalty, as taking pity and compassion forsooth upon man's blood, like a loving and a merciful prince. Another putteth the king in remembrance of certain old and moth-eaten laws, that of long time have not been put in execution, which because no man can remember that they were made, every man hath transgressed. The fines of these laws he counselleth the king to require; for there is no way so profitable, nor more honourable, as the which hath a show and colour of justice. Another adviseth him to forbid many things under great penalties and fines, specially such things as is for the people's profit not be used, and afterwards to dispense for money with them which by this prohibition sustain loss and damage. For by this means the favour of the people is won, and profit riseth two ways. First by taking forfeits of them whom covetousness of gains hath brought in danger of this statute, and also by selling privileges and licences, which the better that the prince is forsooth, the dearer he selleth them; as one that is loath to grant to any private person anything that is against the profit of his people. And therefore may sell none but at an exceeding dear price.

'Another giveth the king counsel to endanger unto his grace the judges of the realm, that he may have them ever on his side, and that they may in every matter dispute and reason for the king's right. Yea, and further to call them into his palace and to require them there to argue and discuss his matters in his own presence. So there shall be no matter of his so openly wrong and unjust, wherein one or other of them, either because he will have something to allege and object, or that he is ashamed to say that which is said already, or else to pick a thank with his prince, will not find some hole open to set a snare in, wherewith to take the contrary part in a trip. Thus whilst the judges cannot agree amongst themselves, reasoning and arguing of that which is plain enough, and bringing the manifest truth in doubt; in the mean season the king may take a fit occasion to understand the law as shall most make for his advantage, whereunto all other for shame or for fear will agree. Then the judges may be bold to pronounce on the king's side. For he that giveth sentence for the king cannot be without a good excuse. For it shall be sufficient for him to have equity on his part, or the bare words of the law, or a written and wrested understanding of the same, or else, which with good and just judges is of greater force than all laws be, the king's indisputable prerogative.

'To conclude, all the counsellors agree and consent together with the rich Crassus, that no abundance of gold can be sufficient for a prince, which must keep and maintain an army: furthermore that a king, though he would, can do nothing unjustly. For all that all men have, yea also the men themselves, be all his. And that every man hath so much of his own as the king's gentleness hath not taken from him. And that it shall be most for the king's advantage that his subjects have very little or nothing in their possession, as whose safeguard doth herein consist, that his people do not wax wanton and wealthy through riches and liberty, because where these things be, there men be not wont patiently to obey hard, unjust, and unlawful commandments; whereas, on the other part, need and poverty doth hold down and keep under stout courages, and maketh them patient perforce, taking from them bold and rebelling stomachs.

'Here again, if I should rise up and boldly affirm that all these counsels be to the king dishonour and reproach, whose honour and safety is more and rather supported and upholden by the wealth and riches of his people than by his own treasures; and if I should declare that the commonalty chooseth their king for their own sake, and not for his sake; to the intent, that through his labour and study they might all live wealthily safe from wrongs and injuries; and that therefore the king ought to take more care for the wealth of his people than for his own wealth, even as the office and duty of a shepherd is, in that he is a shepherd, to feed his sheep rather than himself.

'For as touching this, that they think the defence and maintenance of peace to consist in the poverty of the people, the thing itself showeth that they be far out of the way. For where shall a man find more wrangling, quarrelling, brawling, and chiding, than among beggars? Who be more desirous of new mutations and alterations, than they that be not content with the present state of their life? Or, finally, who be bolder stomached to bring all in a hurly-burly (thereby trusting to get some windfall) than they that have now nothing to lose? And if any king were so smally regarded, and so lightly esteemed, yea, so behated of his subjects, that other ways he could not keep them in awe, but only by open wrongs, by polling and shaving, and by bringing them to beggary, surely it were better for him to forsake his kingdom, than to hold it by this means; whereby though the name of a king be kept, yet the majesty is lost; for it is against the dignity of a king to have rule over beggars, but rather over rich and wealthy men. Of this mind was the hardy and courageous Fabricius, when he said that he had rather be a ruler of rich men than be rich himself. And verily one man to live in pleasure and wealth, whilst all others weep and smart for it, that is the part, not of a king, but of a jailer.

'To be short, as he is a foolish physician that cannot cure his patient's disease unless he cast him in another sickness, so he that cannot amend the lives of his subjects but by taking from them the wealth and commodity of life, he must needs grant that he knoweth not the feat how to government. But let him rather amend his own life, renounce unhonest pleasures, and forsake pride. For these be the chief vices that cause him to run in the contempt or hatred of his people. Let him live of his own, hurting no man. Let him do cost not above his power. Let him restrain wickedness. Let him prevent vices, and take away the occasions of offences by well ordering his subjects, and not by suffering wickedness to increase afterward to be punished. Let him not be too hasty in calling again laws which a custom hath abrogated: specially such as have been long forgotten, and never lacked nor needed. And let him never, under the cloak and pretence of transgression, take such fines and forfeits as no judge will suffer a private person to take, as unjust and full of guile.

'Here if I should bring forth before them the law of the Macariens, which be not far distant from Utopia; whose king the day of his coronation is bound by a solemn oath, that he shall never at any time have in his treasure above a thousand pound of gold or silver. They say a very good king, which took more care for the wealth and commodity of his country than for the enriching of himself, made this law to be a stop and a bar to kings from heaping and hoarding up so much money as might impoverish their people. For he foresaw that this sum of treasure would suffice to support the king in battle against his own people, if they should chance to rebel; and also to maintain his wars against the invasions of his foreign enemies. Again, he perceived the same stock of money to be too little and insufficient to encourage and enable him wrongfully to take away other men's goods: which was the chief cause why the law was made. Another cause was this. He thought that by this provision his people should not lack money wherewith to maintain their daily occupying and chaffer. And seeing the king could not choose but lay out and bestow all that came in above the prescript sum of his stock, he thought he would seek no occasions to do his subjects injury. Such a king shall be feared of evil men, and loved of good men. These, and such other informations, if I should use among men wholly inclined and given to the contrary part, how deaf hearers, think you, should I have?'

'Deaf hearers doubtless' (quoth I), 'and in good faith no marvel. And to be plain with you, truly I cannot allow that such communication shall be used, or such counsel given, as you be sure shall never be regarded nor received. For how can so strange informations be profitable, or how can they be beaten into their heads, whose minds be already prevented with clean contrary persuasions? This school philosophy is not unpleasant among friends in familiar communication, but in the counsels of kings, where great matters be debated and reasoned with great authority, these things have no place.'

'That is it which I meant' (quoth he), 'when I said philosophy had no place among kings.'

'Indeed' (quoth I), 'this school philosophy hath not: which thinketh all things meet for every place. But there is another philosophy more civil, which knoweth, as ye would say, her own stage, and thereafter ordering and behaving herself in the play that she hath in hand, playeth her part accordingly with comeliness, uttering nothing out of due order and fashion. And this is the philosophy that you must use. Or else whilst a comedy of Plautus is playing, and the vile bondmen scoffing and trifling among themselves, if you should suddenly come upon the stage in a philosopher's apparel, and rehearse out of Octavia the place wherein Seneca disputeth with Nero; had it not been better for you to have played the dumb person, than by rehearsing that which served neither for the time nor place, to have made such a tragical comedy or gallimaufry? For by bringing in other stuff that nothing appertaineth to the present matter, you must needs mar and pervert the play that is in hand, though the stuff that you bring be much better. What part soever you have taken upon you, play that as well as you can and make the best of it. And do not therefore disturb and bring out of order the whole matter, because that another, which is merrier and better, cometh to your remembrance.

'So the case standeth in a commonwealth, and so it is in the consultations of kings and princes. If evil opinions and naughty persuasions cannot be utterly and quite plucked out of their hearts, if you cannot even as you would remedy vices which use and custom hath confirmed; yet for this cause you must not leave and forsake the commonwealth. You must not forsake the ship in a tempest, because you cannot rule and keep down the winds. No, nor you must not labour to drive into their heads new and strange informations, which you know well shall be nothing regarded with them that be of clean contrary minds. But you must with a crafty wile and a subtle train study and endeavour yourself, as much as in you lieth, to handle the matter wittily and handsomely for the purpose, and that which you cannot turn to good, so to order it that it be not very bad. For it is not possible for all things to be well, unless all men were good. Which I think will not be yet these good many years.'

'By this means' (quoth he) 'nothing else will be brought to pass, but while that I go about to remedy the madness of others, I should be even as mad as they. For if I would speak such things that be true I must needs speak such things: but as for to speak false things, whether that be a philosopher's part or no I cannot tell, truly it is not my part. Howbeit this communication of mine, though peradventure it may seem unpleasant to them, yet can I not see why it should seem strange, or foolishly new-fangled. If so be that I should speak those things that Plato feigneth in his weal public, or that the Utopians do in theirs, these things, though they were (as they be indeed) better, yet they might seem spoken out of place. Forasmuch as here among us, every man hath his possessions several to himself, and there all things be common.

'But what was in my communication contained, that might not, and ought not, in any place to be spoken? Saving that to them which have thoroughly decreed and determined with themselves to run headlong the contrary way, it cannot be acceptable and pleasant, because it calleth them back and showeth them the jeopardies. Verily, if all things that evil and vicious manners have caused to seem inconvenient and naught should be refused, as things unmeet and reproachful, then we must among Christian people wink at the most part of all those things which Christ taught us, and so straightly forbade them to be winked at, that those things also which He whispered in the ears of His disciples He commanded to be proclaimed in open houses. And yet the most part of them are more dissident from the manners of the world nowadays than my communication was.

'But preachers, sly and wily men, following your counsel (as I suppose), because they saw men evil-willing to frame their manners to Christ's rule, they have wrested and wryed His doctrine, and like a rule of lead have applied it to men's manners; that by some means at the least way, they might agree together. Whereby I cannot see what good they have done, but that men may more sickerly be evil. And I truly should prevail even as little in kings' councils. For either I must say otherwise than they say, and then I were as good to say nothing, or else I must say the same that they say, and (as Mitio saith in Terence) help to further their madness. For that crafty wile and subtle train of yours, I cannot perceive to what purpose it serveth, wherewith you would have me to study and endeavour myself, if all things cannot be made good, yet to handle them wittily and handsomely for the purpose, that as far forth as is possible they may not be very evil. For there is no place to dissemble in, nor to wink in. Naughty counsels must be openly allowed, and very pestilent decrees must be approved. He shall be counted worse than a spy, yea, almost as evil as a traitor, that with a faint heart doth praise evil and noisome decrees.

'Moreover, a man can have no occasion to do good, chancing into the company of them, which will sooner pervert a good man, than be made good themselves; through whose evil company he shall be marred, or else if he remain good and innocent, yet the wickedness and folly of others shall be imputed to him, and laid in his neck. So that it is impossible with that crafty wile and subtle train to turn anything to better.

'Wherefore Plato, by a goodly similitude, declareth why wise men refrain to meddle in the commonwealth. For when they see the people swarm into the streets, and daily wet to the skin with rain, and yet cannot persuade them to go out of the rain, and to take their houses, knowing well that if they should go out to them, they should nothing prevail, nor win aught by it, but with them be wet also in the rain, they do keep themselves within their houses, being content that they be safe themselves, seeing they cannot remedy the folly of the people.

'Howbeit, doubtless, Master More (to speak truly as my mind giveth me), where possessions be private, where money beareth all the stroke, it is hard and almost impossible that there the weal public may justly be governed and prosperously flourish. Unless you think thus: that justice is there executed, where all things come into the hands of evil men, or that prosperity there flourisheth, where all is divided among a few; which few nevertheless do not lead their lives very wealthily, and the residue live miserably, wretchedly, and beggarly.

'Wherefore when I consider with myself and weigh in my mind the wise and godly ordinances of the Utopians, among whom, with very few laws, all things be so well and wealthily ordered, that virtue is had in prize and estimation, and yet all things being there common, every man hath abundance of everything. Again, on the other part, when I compare with them so many nations ever making new laws, yet none of them all well and sufficiently furnished with laws; where every man calleth that he hath gotten his own proper and private goods, where so many new laws daily made be not sufficient for every man to enjoy, defend, and know from another man's that which he calleth his own; which thing the infinite controversies in the law, daily rising, never to be ended, plainly declare to be true.

'These things (I say), when I consider with myself, I hold well with Plato, and do nothing marvel, that he would make no laws for them that refused those laws whereby all men should have and enjoy equal portions of wealth and commodities. For the wise man did easily foresee this to be the one and only way to the wealth of a community, if equality of all things should be brought in and established. Which I think is not possible to be observed where every man's goods be proper and peculiar to himself. For where every man under certain titles and pretences draweth and plucketh to himself as much as he can, so that a few divide among themselves all the whole riches, be there never so much abundance and store, there to the residue is left lack and poverty. And for the most part it chanceth that this latter sort is more worthy to enjoy that state of wealth, than the other be; because the rich men be covetous, crafty, and unprofitable. On the other part, the poor be lowly, simple, and by their daily labour more profitable to the commonwealth than to themselves.

'Thus I do fully persuade myself that no equal and just distribution of things can be made, nor that perfect wealth shall ever be among men, unless this propriety be exiled and banished. But so long as it shall continue, so long shall remain among the most and best part of men the heavy and inevitable burden of poverty and wretchedness. Which, as I grant that it may be somewhat eased so I utterly deny that it can wholly be taken away. For if there were a statute made, that no man should possess above a certain measure of ground, and that no man should have in his stock above a prescript and appointed sum of money; if it were by certain laws decreed, that neither the king should be of too great power, neither the people too haughty and wealthy, and that offices should not be obtained by inordinate suit, or by bribes and gifts; that they should neither be bought nor sold, nor that it should be needful for the officers to be at any cost or charge in their offices; for so occasion is given to them by fraud and ravin to gather up their money again, and by reason of gifts and bribes the offices be given to rich men which should rather have been executed of wise men: by such laws, I say, like as sick bodies that be desperate and past cure, be wont with continual good cherishing to be kept and botched up for a time; so these evils also might be lightened and mitigated. But that they may be perfectly cured, and brought to a good and upright state, it is not to be hoped for whiles every man is master of his own to himself. Yea, and whiles you go about to do your cure of one part, you shall make bigger the sore of another part, so the help of one causeth another's harm; forasmuch as nothing can be given to anyone, unless it be taken from another.'

'But I am of a contrary opinion' (quoth I), 'for methinketh that men shall never there live wealthily where all things be common. For how can there be abundance of goods, or of anything, where every man withdraweth his hand from labour? Whom the regard of his own gains driveth not to work, but the hope that he hath in other men's travails maketh him slothful. Then when they be pricked with poverty, and yet no man can by any law or right defend that for his own, which he hath gotten with the labour of his own hands, shall not there of necessity be continual sedition and bloodshed? Specially the authority and reverence of magistrates being taken away, which, what place it may have with such men among whom is no difference, I cannot devise.'

'I marvel not' (quoth he) 'that you be of this opinion. For you conceive in your mind either none at all, or else a very false image and similitude of this thing. But if you had been with me in Utopia, and had presently seen their fashions and laws, as I did, which lived there five years, and more, and would never have come hence, but only to make that new land known here; then, doubtless, you would grant that you never saw people well ordered, but only there.'

'Surely' (quoth Master Peter) 'it shall be hard for you to make me believe that there is better order in that new land than is here in these countries that we know. For good wits be as well here as there; and I think our commonwealths be ancienter than theirs; wherein long use and experience hath found out many things commodious for man's life, besides that many things here among us have been found by chance, which no wit could ever have devised.'

'As touching the ancientness' (quoth he) 'of commonwealths, then you might better judge, if you had read the histories and chronicles of that land, which if we may believe, cities were there, before men were here. Now what thing soever hitherto by wit hath been devised, or found by chance, that might be as well there as here. But I think verily, though it were so that we did pass them in wit, yet in study, in travail, and in laboursome endeavour they far pass us. For (as their chronicles testify) before our arrival there, they never heard anything of us, whom they call the ultraequinoctials; saving that once, about twelve hundred years ago, a certain ship was lost by the Isle of Utopia which was driven thither by tempest. Certain Romans and Egyptians were cast on land, which after that never went thence.

'Mark now what profit they took of this one occasion through diligence and earnest travail. There was no craft nor science within the Empire of Rome whereof any profit could rise, but they either learned it of these strangers, or else of them taking occasion to search for it, found it out. So great profit was it to them that ever any went thither from hence. But if any like chance before this hath brought any man from thence hither, that is as quite out of remembrance, as this also perchance in time to come shall be forgotten, that ever I was there. And like as they quickly, almost at the first meeting, made their own, whatsoever is among us wealthily devised; so I suppose it would be long before we would receive anything that among them is better instituted than among us. And this I suppose is the chief cause why their commonwealths be wiselier governed, and do flourish in more wealth than ours, though we neither in wit nor riches be their inferiors.'

'Therefore, gentle Master Raphael' (quoth I), 'I pray you and beseech you describe unto us the island. And study not to be short; but declare largely in order their grounds, their rivers, their cities, their people, their manners, their ordinances, their laws, and, to be short, all things that you shall think us desirous to know. And you shall think us desirous to know whatsoever we know not yet.'

'There is nothing' (quoth he) 'that I will do gladlier. For all these things I have fresh in mind. But the matter requireth leisure.'

'Let us go in, therefore' (quoth I), 'to dinner, afterward we will bestow the time at our pleasure.'

'Content' (quoth he) 'be it.'

So we went in and dined. When dinner was done we came into the same place again, and sat us down upon the same bench, commanding our servants that no man should trouble us. Then I and Master Peter Giles desired Master Raphael to perform his promise. He, therefore, seeing us desirous and willing to hearken to him, when he had sat still and paused a little while, musing and bethinking himself, thus he began to speak.

THE END OF THE FIRST BOOK

THE SECOND BOOK
OF THE COMMUNICATION OF RAPHAEL
HYTHLODAY, CONCERNING THE BEST
STATE OF A COMMONWEALTH:
CONTAINING THE DESCRIPTION OF
UTOPIA, WITH A LARGE DECLARATION OF
THE POLITIC GOVERNMENT, AND OF ALL
THE GOOD LAWS AND ORDERS OF
THE SAME ISLAND

The Description of Utopia

The Island of Utopia containeth in breadth in the middle part of it (for there it is broadest) two hundred miles. Which breadth continueth through the most part of the land, saving that by little and little it cometh in and waxeth narrower towards both the ends. Which fetching about a circuit or compass of five hundred miles, do fashion the whole island like to the new moon. Between these two corners the sea runneth in, dividing them asunder by the distance of eleven miles or thereabouts, and there surmounteth into a large and wide sea, which by reason that the land on every side compasseth it about, and sheltereth it from the winds, is not rough, nor mounteth not with great waves, but almost floweth quietly, not much unlike a great standing pool; and maketh well-nigh all the space within the belly of the land in manner of a haven; and to the great commodity of the inhabitants receiveth in ships towards every part of the land. The forefronts or frontiers of the two corners, what with fords and shelves, and what with rocks, be very jeopardous and dangerous. In the middle distance between them both standeth up above the water a great rock, which therefore is nothing perilous because it is in sight. Upon the top of this rock is a fair and a strong tower built, which they hold with a garrison of men. Other rocks there be lying hid under the water, which therefore be dangerous. The channels be known only to themselves. And therefore it seldom chanceth that any stranger, unless he be guided by an Utopian, can come into this haven. Insomuch that they themselves could scarcely enter without jeopardy, but that their way is directed and ruled by certain landmarks standing on the shore. By turning, translating, and removing these marks into other places they may destroy their enemies' navies, be they ever so many. The outside or utter circuit of the land is also full of havens, but the landing is so surely fenced, what by nature, and what by workmanship of man's hand, that a few defenders may drive back many armies.

Howbeit as they say, and as the fashion of the place itself doth partly show, it was not ever compassed about with the sea. But King Utopus, whose name, as conqueror, the island beareth (for before his time it was called Abraxa), which also brought the rude and wild people to that excellent perfection in all good fashions, humanity, and civil gentleness, wherein they now go beyond all the people of the world; even at his first arriving and entering upon the land, forthwith obtaining the victory, caused fifteen miles' space of uplandish ground, where the sea had no passage, to be cut and digged up, and so brought the sea round about the land. He set to this work not only the inhabitants of the island (because they should not think it done in contumely and despite), but also all his own soldiers. Thus the work being divided into so great a number of workmen, was with exceeding marvellous speed dispatched. Insomuch that the borderers, which at the first began to mock and to jest at this vain enterprise, then turned their derision to marvel at the success, and to fear.

There be in the island fifty-four large and fair cities, or shire towns, agreeing altogether in one tongue, in like manners, institutions, and laws. They be all set and situated alike, and in all points fashioned alike, as far north as the place or plot suffereth. Of these cities they that be nighest together be twenty-four miles asunder. Again there is none of them distant from the next above one day's journey on foot.

There come yearly to Amaurote out of every city three old men, wise and well experienced, there to entreat and debate of the common matters of the land. For this city (because it standeth just in the middle of the island, and is therefore most meet for the ambassadors of all parts of the realm) is taken for the chief and head city. The precincts and bounds of the shires be so commodiously appointed out, and set forth for the cities, that none of them all hath of any side less than twenty miles of ground, and of some side also much more, as of that part where the cities be of farther distance asunder. None of the cities desire to enlarge the bounds and limits of their shires. For they count themselves rather the good husbands, than the owners of their lands.

They have in the country in all parts of the shire houses or farms built, well appointed and furnished with all sorts of instruments and tools belonging to husbandry. These houses be inhabited of the citizens, which come thither to dwell by course. No household or farm in the country hath fewer than forty persons, men and women, besides two bondmen, which be all under the rule and order of the good-man and the good-wife of the house, being both very sage, discreet, and ancient persons. And every thirty farms or families have one head ruler, which is called a Philarch, being as it were, a head bailiff. Out of every one of these families or farms cometh every year into the city twenty persons which have continued two years before in the country. In their place so many fresh be sent thither out of the city, who, of them that have been there a year already, and be therefore expert and cunning in husbandry, shall be instructed and taught. And they the next year shall teach other. This order is used for fear that either scarceness of victuals, or some other like incommodity should chance, through lack of knowledge, if they should be altogether new, and fresh, and unexpert in husbandry. This manner and fashion of yearly changing and renewing the occupiers of husbandry, though it be solemn and customably used, to the intent that no man shall be constrained against his will to continue long in that hard and sharp kind of life, yet many of them have such a pleasure and delight in husbandry, that they obtain a longer space of years. These husbandmen plough and till the ground, and breed up cattle, and provide and make ready wood, which they carry to the city either by land, or by water, as they may most conveniently.

They bring up a great multitude of pulleyn, and that by a marvellous policy. For the hens do not sit upon the eggs, but by keeping them in a certain equal heat they bring life into them, and hatch them. The chickens, as soon as they become out of the shell, follow men and women instead of the hens.

They bring up very few horses, nor none but very fierce ones; and that for none other use or purpose, but only to exercise their youth in riding and feats of arms. For oxen be put to all the labour of ploughing and drawing. Which they grant to be not so good as horses at a sudden brunt, and (as we say) at a dead lift, but yet they hold opinion, that oxen will abide and suffer much more labour, pain, and hardness, than horses will. And they think that oxen be not in danger and subject unto so many diseases, and that they be kept and maintained with much less cost and charge; and, finally, that they be good for meat when they be past labour.

They sow corn only for bread. For their drink is either wine made of grapes, or else of apples, or pears, or else it is clear water. And many times mead made of honey or liquorice sodden in water, for thereof they have great store. And though they know certainly (for they know it perfectly indeed) how much victuals the city with the whole country or shire round about it doth spend, yet they sow much more corn, and breed up much more cattle, than serveth for their own use, parting the overplus among their borderers. Whatsoever necessary things be lacking in the country, all such stuff they fetch out of the city; where without any exchange they easily obtain it of the magistrates of the city. For every month many of them go into the city on the holy day. When their harvest day draweth near, and is at hand, then the Philarchs, which be the head officers and bailiffs of husbandry, send word to the magistrates of the city what number of harvestmen is needful to be sent to them out of the city. The which company of harvestmen being ready at the day appointed, almost in one fair day dispatcheth all the harvest work.

Of the Cities and namely of Amaurote

As for their cities, whoso knoweth one of then, knoweth them all: they be all so like one to another, as far forth as the nature of the place permitteth. I will describe, therefore, to you one or other of them, for it skilleth not greatly which; but which rather than Amaurote? Of them all this is the worthiest and of most dignity. For the residue acknowledge it for the head city, because there is the council-house. Nor to me any of them all is better beloved, as wherein I lived five whole years together. The city of Amaurote standeth upon the side of a low hill, in fashion almost four-square. For the breadth of it beginneth a little beneath the top of the hill, and still continueth by the space of two miles, until it come to the river of Anyder. The length of it, which lieth by the riverside, is somewhat more.

The river of Anyder riseth four and twenty miles above Amaurote out of a little spring. But being increased by other small rivers and brooks that run into it, and among other two somewhat big ones, before the city it is half a mile broad, and farther broader. And forty miles beyond the city it falleth into the ocean sea. By all that space that lieth between the sea and the city, and certain miles also above the city, the water ebbeth and floweth six hours together with a swift tide. When the sea floweth in, for the length of thirty miles, it filleth all the Anyder with salt water, and driveth back the fresh water of the river. And somewhat further it changeth the sweetness of the fresh water with saltness. But a little beyond that the river waxeth sweet, and runneth forby the city fresh and pleasant. And when the sea ebbeth and goeth back again, the fresh water followeth it almost even to the very fall into the sea.

There goeth a bridge over the river made not of piles or of timber, but of stonework, with gorgeous and substantial arches at that part of the city that is farthest from the sea; to the intent that ships may pass along forby all the side of the city without let.

They have also another river which, indeed, is not very great. But it runneth gently and pleasantly. For it riseth even out of the same hill that the city standeth upon, and runneth down a slope through the midst of the city into Anyder. And because it riseth a little without the city, the Amaurotians have enclosed the head-spring of it with strong fences and bulwarks, and so have joined it to the city. This is done to the intent that the water should not be stopped, nor turned away, nor poisoned, if their enemies should chance to come upon them. From thence the water is derived and conveyed down in channels of brick divers ways into the lower parts of the city. Where that cannot be done, by reason that the place will not suffer it, there they gather the rain-water in great cisterns, which doeth them as good service.

The city is compassed about with a high and thick stone wall full of turrets and bulwarks. A dry ditch, but deep, and broad, and overgrown with bushes, briers, and thorns, goeth about three sides or quarters of the city. To the fourth side the river itself serveth for a ditch. The streets be appointed and set forth very commodious and handsome, both for carriage, and also against the winds. The houses be of fair and gorgeous building, and on the street side they stand joined together in a long row, through the whole street, without any partition or separation. The streets be twenty feet broad. On the back side of the houses, through the whole length of the street, lie large gardens enclosed round about with the back part of the streets. Every house hath two doors, one into the street, and a postern door on the back side into the garden. These doors be made with two leaves, never locked nor bolted, so easy to be opened, that they will follow the least drawing of a finger, and shut again alone. Whoso will, may go in, for there is nothing within the houses that is private, or any man's own. And every tenth year they change their houses by lot.

They set great store by their gardens. In them they have vineyards, all manner of fruit, herbs, and flowers, so pleasant, so well furnished, and so finely kept, that I never saw thing more fruitful nor better trimmed in any place. Their study and diligence herein cometh not only of pleasure, but also of a certain strife and contention that is between street and street concerning the trimming, husbanding, and furnishing of their gardens; every man for his own part. And verily you shall not lightly find in all the city anything that is more commodious, either for the profit of the citizens or for pleasure. And, therefore, it may seem that the first founder of the city minded nothing so much as these gardens. For they say that King Utopus himself, even at the first beginning, appointed and drew forth the platform of the city into this fashion and figure that it hath now, but the gallant garnishing, and the beautiful setting forth of it, whereunto he saw that one man's age would not suffice: that he left to his posterity. For their chronicles, which they keep written with all diligent circumspection, containing the history of one thousand seven hundred and sixty years, even from the first conquest of the island, record and witness that the houses in the beginning were very low, and like homely cottages or poor shepherd houses, made, at all adventures, of every rude piece of timber that came first to hand, with mud walls, and ridged roofs thatched over with straw. But now the houses be curiously built, after a gorgeous and gallant sort, with three storeys, one over another. The outsides of the walls be made either of hard flint, or of plaster, or else of brick, and the inner sides be well strengthened with timber work. The roofs be plain and flat, covered with a certain kind of plaster that is of no cost, and yet so tempered that no fire can hurt or perish it, and withstandeth the violence of the weather better than any lead. They keep the wind out of their windows with glass, for it is there much used, and some here also with fine linen cloth dipped in oil or amber, and that for two commodities. For by this means more light cometh in, and the wind is better kept out.

Of the Magistrates

Every thirty families or farms choose them yearly an officer, which in their old language is called the Syphogrant, and by a newer name the Philarch. Every ten Syphogrants, with all their thirty families, be under an officer which was once called the Tranibor, now the chief Philarch. Moreover, as concerning the election of the prince, all the Syphogrants, which be in number two hundred, first be sworn to choose him whom they think most meet and expedient. Then by a secret election, they name prince one of those four whom the people before named unto them. For out of the four quarters of the city there be four chosen, out of every quarter one, to stand for the election; which be put up to the council. The prince's office continueth all his lifetime, unless he be deposed or put down for suspicion of tyranny. They choose the Tranibors yearly, but lightly they change them not. All the other officers be but for one year. The Tranibors every third day, and sometimes, if need be, oftener, come into the council-house with the prince. Their counsel is concerning the commonwealth. If there be any controversies among the commoners, which be very few, they dispatch and end them by and by. They take ever two Syphogrants to them in counsel, and every day a new couple. And it is provided that nothing touching the commonwealth shall be confirmed and ratified, unless it have been reasoned of and debated three days in the council before it be decreed.

It is death to have any consultation for the commonwealth out of the council, or the place of the common election. This statute, they say, was made to the intent, that the prince and Tranibors might not easily conspire together to oppress the people by tyranny, and to change the state of the weal public. Therefore matters of great weight and importance be brought to the election-house of the Syphogrants, which open the matter to their families. And afterwards, when they have consulted among themselves, they show their device to the

council. Sometimes the matter is brought before the council of the
whole island.

Furthermore, this custom also the council useth, to dispute or
reason of no matter the same day that it is first proposed or put forth,
but to defer it to the next sitting of the council. Because that no man
when he hath rashly there spoken that cometh to his tongue's end,
shall then afterward rather study for reasons wherewith to defend and
maintain his first foolish sentence, than for the commodity of the
commonwealth; as one rather willing the harm or hindrance of the
weal public than any loss or diminution of his own existimation. And
as one that would be ashamed (which is a very foolish shame) to be
counted anything at the first overseen in the matter; who at the first
ought to have spoken rather wisely, than hastily or rashly.

Of Sciences, Crafts and Occupations

Husbandry is a science common to them all in general, both men and women, wherein they be all expert and cunning. In this they be all instructed even from their youth; partly in their schools with traditions and precepts, and partly in the country nigh the city, brought up as it were in playing, not only beholding the use of it, but by occasion of exercising their bodies practising it also.

Besides husbandry, which (as I said) is common to them all, every one of them learneth one or other several and particular science, as his own proper craft. That is most commonly either clothworking in wool or flax, or masonry, of the smith's craft, or the carpenter's science. For there is none other occupation that any number to speak of doth use there. For their garments, which throughout all the island be of one fashion (saving that there is a difference between the man's garment and the woman's, between the married and the unmarried), and this one continueth for evermore unchanged, seemly and comely to the eye, no let to the moving and welding of the body, also fit both for winter and summer: as for these garments (I say) every family maketh their own. But of the other foresaid crafts every man learneth one. And not only the men, but also the women. But the women, as the weaker sort, be put to the easier crafts; as to work wool and flax. The more laboursome sciences be committed to the men. For the most part every man is brought up in his father's craft. For most commonly they be naturally thereto bent and inclined. But if a man's mind stand to any other, he is by adoption put into a family of that occupation, which he doth most fantasy. Whom not only his father, but also the magistrates do diligently look to, that he be put to a discreet and an honest householder. Yea, and if any person, when he hath learned one craft, be desirous to learn also another, he is likewise suffered and permitted.

When he hath learned both, he occupieth whether he will; unless
the city have more need of the one than of the other. The chief and
almost the only office of the Syphogrants is, to see and take heed that
no man sit idle, but that every one apply his own craft with earnest
diligence; and yet for all that, not to be wearied, from early in the
morning to late in the evening, with continual work, like labouring
and toiling beasts. For this is worse than the miserable and wretched
condition of bondmen, which nevertheless is almost everywhere the
life of workmen and artificers, saving in Utopia.

For they, dividing the day and the night into twenty-four just hours,
appoint and assign only six of those hours to work; three before noon,
upon the which they go straight to dinner; and after dinner, when they
have rested two hours, then they work three hours, and upon that
they go to supper. About eight of the clock in the evening (counting
one of the clock at the first hour after noon) they go to bed; eight
hours they give to sleep. All the void time, that is between the hours of
work, sleep, and meat, that they be suffered to bestow, every man as
he liketh best himself. Not to the intent that they should misspend this
time in riot or slothfulness; but being then licensed from the labour of
their own occupations, to bestow the time well and thriftily upon
some other science, as shall please them. For it is a solemn custom
there to have lectures daily early in the morning; where to be present
they only be constrained that be namely chosen and appointed to
learning. Howbeit a great multitude of every sort of people, both men
and women, go to hear lectures, some one and some another, as every
man's nature is inclined. Yet, this notwithstanding, if any man had
rather bestow this time upon his own occupation (as it chanceth in
many, whose minds rise not in the contemplation of any science
liberal) he is not letted nor prohibited, but is also praised and
commended, as profitable to the commonwealth.

After supper they bestow one hour in play; in summer in their
gardens, in winter in their common halls where they dine and sup.
There they exercise themselves in music, or else in honest and
wholesome communication. Dice-play, and such other foolish and
pernicious games they know not. But they use two games not much
unlike the chess. The one is the battle of numbers, wherein one
number stealeth away another. The other is wherein vices fight with
virtues, as it were in battle array, or a set field. In the which game is
very properly showed both the strife and discord that vices have

among themselves, and again their unity and concord against virtues; and also what vices be repugnant to what virtues: with what power and strength they assail them openly; by what wiles and subtlety they assault them secretly: with what help and aid the virtues resist, and overcome the puissance of the vices; by what craft they frustrate their purposes: and finally by what sleight or means the one getteth the victory.

But here lest you be deceived, one thing you must look more narrowly upon. For seeing they bestow but six hours in work, perchance you may think that the lack of some necessary things hereof may ensue. But this is nothing so. For that small time is not only enough, but also too much for the store and abundance of all things that be requisite, either for the necessity or commodity of life. The which thing you also shall perceive, if you weigh and consider with yourselves how great a part of the people in other countries liveth idle. First, almost all women, which be the half of the whole number; or else if the women be somewhere occupied, there most commonly in their stead the men be idle. Besides this, how great and how idle a company is there of priests and religious men, as they call them? Put thereto all rich men, specially all landed men, which commonly be called gentlemen, and noblemen. Take into this number also their servants: I mean all that flock of stout bragging rush-bucklers. Joined to them also sturdy and valiant beggars, cloaking their idle life under the colour of some disease or sickness. And truly you shall find them much fewer than you thought, by whose labour all these things are wrought, that in men's affairs are now daily used and frequented. Now consider with yourself, of those few that do work, how few be occupied in necessary works. For where money beareth all the swing, there many vain and superfluous occupations must needs be used, to serve only for riotous superfluity and unhonest pleasure. For the same multitude that now is occupied in work, if they were divided into so few occupations as the necessary use of nature requireth; in so great plenty of things as then of necessity would ensue, doubtless the prices would be too little for the artificers to maintain their livings. But if all these that be now busied about unprofitable occupations, with all the whole flock of them that live idly and slothfully, which consume and waste every one of them more of these things that come by other men's labour, than two of the workmen themselves do: if all these (I say) were set to profitable occupations, you easily perceive how little time would be enough, yea and too much, to store us with all things that many be requisite either for necessity or for commodity, yea or for pleasure, so that the same pleasure be true and natural.

And this in Utopia the thing itself maketh manifest and plain. For there in all the city, with the whole country or shire adjoining to it, scarcely five hundred persons of all the whole number of men and women, that be neither too old nor too weak to work, be licensed and discharged from labour. Among them be the Syphogrants (who though they be by the laws exempt and privileged from labour) yet they exempt not themselves; to the intent that they may the rather by their example provoke others to work. The same vacation from labour do they also enjoy to whom the people, persuaded by the commendation of the priests and secret election of the Syphogrants, have given a perpetual licence from labour to learning. But if any one of them prove not according to the expectation and hope of him conceived, he is forthwith plucked back to the company of artificers. And contrariwise, often it chanceth that a handicraftsman doth so earnestly bestow his vacant and spare hours in learning, and through diligence so profiteth therein, that he is taken from his handy occupation, and promoted to the company of the learned. Out of this order of the learned be chosen ambassadors, priests, Tranibors, and finally the prince himself. Whom they in their old tongue call Barzanes, and by a newer name, Ademus. The residue of the people being neither idle, nor yet occupied about unprofitable exercises, it may be easily judged in how few hours how much good work by them may be done and dispatched, towards those things that I have spoken of.

This commodity they have also above others, that in the most part of necessary occupations they need not so much work as other nations do. For first of all the building or repairing of houses asketh everywhere so many men's continual labour, because that the unthrifty heir suffereth the houses that his father built in continuance of time to fall in decay. So that which he might have upholden with little cost, his successor is constrained to build it again anew, to his great charge. Yea, many times also the house that stood one man in much money, another is of so nice and so delicate a mind that he setteth nothing by it. And it being neglected, and therefore shortly falling into ruin, he buildeth up another in another place with no less cost and charge. But among the Utopians, where all things be set in a good order, and the commonwealth in a good stay, it very seldom chanceth that they choose a new plot to build a house upon. And they do not only find speedy and quick remedies for present faults, but also prevent them that be like to fall. And by this means their houses continue and last very long with little labour and small reparations; in so much that this kind of workmen sometimes have almost nothing to do. But that they be commanded to hew timber at home, and to square and trim up stones, to the intent that if any work chance, it may the speedier rise.

Now, sir, in their apparel, mark (I pray you) how few workmen they need. First of all, whilst they be at work, they be covered homely with leather or skins, that will last seven years. When they go forth abroad they cast upon them a cloak, which hideth the other homely apparel. These cloaks throughout the whole island be all of one colour, and that is the natural colour of the wool. They therefore do not only spend much less woollen cloth than is spent in other countries, but also the same standeth them in much less cost. But linen cloth is made with less labour, and is therefore had more in use. But in linen cloth only whiteness, in woollen only cleanliness, is regarded. As for the smallness or fineness of the thread, that is nothing passed for. And this is the cause wherefor in other places four or five cloth gowns of divers colours, and as many silk coats, be not enough for one man. Yea, and if he be of the delicate and nice sort, ten be too few; whereas there one garment will serve a man most commonly two years. For why should he desire more? Seeing if he had them, he should not be the better happed or covered from cold, neither in his apparel any whit the comelier.

Wherefore, seeing they be all exercised in profitable occupations, and that few artificers in the same crafts be sufficient, this is the cause that, plenty of all things being among them, they do sometimes bring forth an innumerable company of people to amend the highways, if any be broken. Many times also, when they have no such work to be occupied about, an open proclamation is made, that they shall bestow fewer hours in work. For the magistrates do not exercise their citizens against their wills in unneedful labours. For why, in the institution of that weal public, this end is only and chiefly pretended and minded, that what time may possibly be spared from the necessary occupations and affairs of the commonwealth, all that the citizens should withdraw from the bodily service to the free liberty of the mind and garnishing of the same. For herein they suppose the felicity of this life to consist.

Of their Living and Mutual
Conversation Together

But now will I declare how the citizens use themselves one towards another; what familiar occupying and entertainment there is among the people, and what fashion they use in the distribution of everything. First the city consisteth of families, the families most commonly be made of kindreds. For the women, when they be married at a lawful age, they go into their husbands' houses. But the male children, with all the whole male offspring, continue still in their own family and be governed of the eldest and ancientest father, unless he dote for age; for then the next to him in age is placed in his room.

But to the intent the prescript number of the citizens should neither decrease nor above measure increase, it is ordained that no family, which in every city be six thousand in the whole, besides them of the country, shall at once have fewer children of the age of fourteen years or thereabout than ten or more than sixteen, for of children under this age no number can be prescribed or appointed. This measure or number is easily observed and kept, by putting them that in fuller families be above the number into families of smaller increase. But if chance be that in the whole city the store increase above the just number, therewith they fill up the lack of other cities.

But if so be that the multitude throughout the whole island pass and exceed the due number, then they choose out of every city certain citizens, and build up a town under their own laws in the next land where the inhabitants have much waste and unoccupied ground, receiving also of the same country people to them, if they will join and dwell with them. They thus joining and dwelling together do easily agree in one fashion of living, and that to the great wealth of both the peoples. For they so bring the matter about by their laws, that the ground which before was neither good nor profitable for the one nor for the other, is now sufficient and fruitful enough for them both. But if the inhabitants of that land will not dwell with them to be ordered by their laws, then they drive them out of those bounds which they have limited and appointed out for themselves. And if they resist and rebel, then they make war against them. For they count this the most just cause of war, when any people holdeth a piece of ground void and vacant to no good nor profitable use, keeping others from the use and possession of it, which notwithstanding by the law of nature ought thereof to be nourished and relieved. If any chance do so much diminish the number of any of their cities that it cannot be filled up again, without the diminishing of the just number of the other cities (which they say chanced but twice since the beginning of the land through a great pestilent plague), then they fulfil and make up the number with citizens fetched out of their own foreign towns, for they had rather suffer their foreign towns to decay and perish, than any city of their own island to be diminished.

But now again to the conversation of the citizens among themselves. The eldest (as I said) ruleth the family. The wives be ministers to their husbands, the children to their parents, and, to be short, the younger to their elders. Every city is divided into four equal parts or quarters. In the midst of every quarter there is a market-place of all manner of things. Thither the works of every family be brought into certain houses. And every kind of thing is laid up several in barns or storehouses. From thence the father of every family, or every householder, fetcheth whatsoever he and his hath need of, and carrieth it away with him without money, without exchange, without any gage, pawn, or pledge. For why should anything be denied unto him? Seeing there is abundance of all things, and that it is not to be feared lest any man will ask more than he needeth. For why should it be thought that that man would ask more than enough which is sure never to lack? Certainly in all kinds of living creatures either fear of lack doth cause covetousness and raven, or in man only pride, which counteth it a glorious thing to pass and excel others in the superfluous and vain ostentation of things. The which kind of vice among the Utopians can have no place.

Next to the market-places that I spake of, stand meat markets; whither be brought not only all sorts of herbs, and the fruits of trees, with bread, but also fish, and all manner of four-footed beasts and wild-fowl that be man's meat. But first the filthiness and odour thereof is clean washed away in the running river without the city, in places appointed meet for the same purpose. From thence the beasts be brought in killed, and clean washed by the hands of their bondmen. For they permit not their free citizens to accustom themselves to the killing of beasts, through the use whereof they think clemency, the gentlest affection of our nature, by little and little to decay and perish. Neither they suffer anything that is filthy, loathsome, or uncleanly, to be brought into the city, lest the air by the stench thereof, infected and corrupt, should cause pestilent diseases.

Moreover, every street hath certain great large halls set in equal distance one from another, every one known by a several name. In these halls dwell the Syphogrants. And to every one of the same halls be appointed thirty families, on either side fifteen. The stewards of every hall at a certain hour come in to the meat markets, where they receive meat according to the number of their halls.

But first, and chiefly of all, respect is had to the sick, that be cured in the hospitals. For in the circuit of the city, a little without the walls, they have four hospitals, so big, so wide, so ample, and so large, that they may seem four little towns, which were devised of that bigness partly to the intent the sick, be they never so many in number, should not lie too throng or strait, and, therefore, uneasily and incommodiously; and partly that they which were taken and holden with contagious diseases, such as be wont by infection to creep from one to another, might be laid apart far from the company of the residue. These hospitals be so well appointed, and with all things necessary to health so furnished, and, moreover, so diligent attendance through the continual presence of cunning physicians is given, that though no man be sent thither against his will, yet, notwithstanding, there is no sick person in all the city that had not rather lie there than at home in his own house.

When the steward of the sick hath received such meats as the physicians have prescribed, then the best is equally divided among the halls, according to the company of every one, saving that there is had a respect to the prince, the bishop, the Tranibors, and to ambassadors, and all strangers, if there be any, which be very few and seldom. But they also, when they be there, have certain several houses appointed and prepared for them.

To these halls at the set hours of dinner and supper cometh all the whole Syphogranty or ward, warned by the noise of a brazen trumpet; except such as be sick in the hospitals, or else in their own houses.

Howbeit no man is prohibited or forbid, after the halls be served, to fetch home meat, out of the market to his own house, for they know that no man will do it without a cause reasonable. For though no man be prohibited to dine at home, yet no man doth it willingly, because it is counted a point of small honesty. And also it were a folly to take the pain to dress a bad dinner at home, when they may be welcome to good and fine fare so nigh hand at the hall. In this hall all vile service, all slavery and drudgery, with all laboursome toil and base business, is done by bondmen. But the women of every family by course have the office and charge of cookery for setting and dressing the meat, and ordering all things thereto belonging. They sit at three tables or more, according to the number of their company. The men sit upon the bench next the wall, and the women against them on the other side of the table, that if any sudden evil should chance to them as many times happeneth to women with child, they may rise without trouble or disturbance of anybody, and go thence into the nursery.

The nurses sit several along with their young sucklings in a certain parlour appointed and deputed to the same purpose, never without fire and clean water, nor yet without cradles, that when they will they may lay down the young infants, and at their pleasure take them out of their swathing clothes, and hold them to the fire, and refresh them with play. Every mother is nurse to her own child, unless either death or sickness be the let. When that chanceth, the wives of the Syphogrants quickly provide a nurse. And that is not hard to be done. For they that can do it, prefer themselves to no service so gladly as to that. Because that there this kind of pity is much praised: and the child that is nourished, ever after taketh his nurse for his own natural mother. Also among the nurses sit all the children that be under the age of five years. All the other children of both kinds, as well boys as girls, that be under the age of marriage, do either serve at the tables, or else if they be too young thereto, yet they stand by with marvellous silence. That which is given to them from the table they eat, and other several dinner-time they have none.

The Syphogrant and his wife sit in the midst of the high table, forasmuch as that is counted the honourablest place, and because from thence all the whole company is in their sight. For that table standeth overthwart the over end of the hall. To them be joined two of the ancientest and eldest. For at every table they sit four at a mess. But if there be a church standing in that Syphogranty or ward, then the priest and his wife sitteth with the Syphogrant as chief in the company. On both sides of them sit young men, and next unto them again old men. And thus throughout all the house equal of age be set together, and yet be mixed and matched with unequal ages. This, they say, was ordained, to the intent that the sage gravity and reverence of the elders should keep the youngers from wanton licence of words and behaviour. Forasmuch as nothing can be so secretly spoken or done at the table, but either they that sit on the one side or on the other must needs perceive it. The dishes be not set down in order from the first place, but all the old men (whose places be marked with some special token to be known) be first served of their meat, and then the residue equally. The old men divide their dainties as they think best to the younger on each side of them. Thus the elders be not defrauded of their due honour, and, nevertheless, equal commodity cometh to every one.

They begin every dinner and supper of reading something that pertaineth to good manners and virtue. But it is short, because no man shall be grieved therewith. Hereof the elders take occasion of honest communication, but neither sad nor unpleasant. Howbeit they do not spend all the whole dinner-time themselves with long and tedious talks, but they gladly hear also the young men; yea, and purposely provoke them to talk, to the intent that they may have a proof of every man's wit, and towardness or disposition to virtue, which commonly in the liberty of feasting doth show and utter itself. Their dinners be very short; but their suppers be somewhat longer; because that after dinner followeth labour, after supper sleep and natural rest, which they think to be of more strength and efficacy to wholesome and healthful digestion. No supper is passed without music. Nor their banquets lack no conceits nor junkets. They burn sweet gums and spices for perfumes and pleasant smells, and sprinkle about sweet ointments and waters, yea, they leave nothing undone that maketh for the cheering of the company. For they be much inclined to this opinion: to think no kind of pleasure forbidden, whereof cometh no harm.

Thus, therefore, and after this sort they live together in the city, but in the country they that dwell alone far from any neighbours, do dine and sup at home in their own houses. For no family there lacketh any kind of victuals, as from whom cometh all that the citizens eat and live by.

Of their Journeying or Travelling Abroad

with divers other matters cunningly reasoned and wittily discussed

But if any be desirous to visit either their friends dwelling in another city, or to see the place itself, they easily obtain licence of their Syphogrants and Tranibors, unless there be some profitable let. No man goeth out alone, but a company is sent forth together with their prince's letters, which do testify that they have licence to go that journey, and prescribeth also the day of their return. They have a wagon given them, with a common bondman, which driveth the oxen and taketh charge of them. But unless they have women in their company, they send home the wagon again, as an impediment and a let. And though they carry nothing forth with them, yet in all their journey they lack nothing. For wheresoever they come, they be at home. If they tarry in a place longer than one day, then there every one of them falleth to his own occupation, and be very gently entertained of the workmen and companies of the same crafts. If any man of his own head, and without leave, walk out of his precinct and bounds, taken without the prince's letters, he is brought again for a fugitive or a runaway with great shame and rebuke, and is sharply punished. If he be taken in that fault again, he is punished with bondage.

If any be desirous to walk abroad into the fields, or into the country that belongeth to the same city that he dwelleth in, obtaining the goodwill of his father and the consent of his wife, he is not prohibited. But into what part of the country soever he cometh he hath no meat given him until he hath wrought out his forenoon's task, or dispatched so much work as there is wont to be wrought before supper. Observing this law and condition, he may go whither he will within the bounds of his own city. For he shall be no less profitable to the city than if he were within it.

Now you see how little liberty they have to loiter: how they can have no cloak or pretence to idleness. There be neither wine-taverns, nor ale-houses, nor stews, nor any occasion of vice or wickedness, no lurking corners, no places of wicked counsels or unlawful assemblies. But they be in the present sight, and under the eyes of every man. So that of necessity they must either apply their accustomed labours, or else recreate themselves with honest and laudable pastimes.

This fashion and trade of life, being used among the people, it cannot be chosen, but that they must of necessity have store and plenty of all things. And seeing they be all thereof partners equally, therefore can no man there be poor or needy. In the council of Amaurote, whither, as I said, every city sendeth three men apiece yearly, as soon as it is perfectly known of what things there is in every place plenty, and, again, what things be scant in any place; incontinent the lack of the one is performed and filled up with the abundance of the other. And this they do freely without any benefit, taking nothing again of them to whom the things is given, but those cities that have given of their store to any other city that lacketh, requiring nothing again of the same city, do take such things as they lack of another city, to the which they gave nothing. So the whole island is, as it were, one family or household.

But when they have made sufficient provision of store for themselves (which they think not done, until they have provided for two years following, because of the uncertainty of the next year's proof), then of those things whereof they have abundance they carry forth into other countries great plenty: as grain, honey, wool, flax, wood, madder, purple-dyed fells, wax, tallow, leather, and living beasts. And the seventh part of all these things they give frankly and freely to the poor of that country. The residue they sell at a reasonable and mean price.

By this trade of traffic or merchandise, they bring into their own country, not only great plenty of gold and silver, but also all such things as they lack at home, which is almost nothing but iron. And by reason they have long used this trade, now they have more abundance of these things than any man will believe. Now, therefore, they care not whether they sell for ready money, or else upon trust to be paid at a day, and to have the most part in debts. But in so doing they never follow the credence of private men, but the assurance or warranty of the whole city, by instruments and writings made in that behalf accordingly. When the day of payment is come and expired, the city gathereth up the debt of the private debtors, and putteth it into the common box, and so long hath the use and profit of it, until the Utopians their creditors demand it. The most part of it they never ask. For that thing which is to them no profit, to take it from others to whom it is profitable they think it no right nor conscience.

But if the case so stand, that they must lend part of that money to another people, then they require their debt; or when they have war. For the which purpose only they keep at home all the treasure which they have, to be helped and secured by it either in extreme jeopardies or in sudden dangers, but especially and chiefly to hire therewith, and that for unreasonable great wages, strange soldiers. For they had rather put strangers in jeopardy than their own countrymen; knowing that for money enough, their enemies themselves many times may be bought or sold, or else through treason be set together by the ears among themselves. For this cause they keep an inestimable treasure. But yet not as a treasure; but so they have it, and use it, as in good faith I am ashamed to show, fearing that my words shall not be believed. And this I have more cause to fear, for that I know how difficultly and hardly I myself would have believed another man telling the same, if I had not presently seen it with mine own eyes. For it must needs be, that how far a thing is dissonant and disagreeing from the guise and trade of the hearers, so far shall it be out of their belief. Howbeit, a wise and indifferent esteemer of things will not greatly marvel perchance, seeing all their other laws and customs do so much differ from ours, if the use also of gold and silver among them be applied rather to their own fashions than to ours. I mean in that they occupy not money themselves, but keep it for that chance, which as it may happen, so it may be that it shall never come to pass.

In the meantime gold and silver, whereof money is made, they do so use, as none of them doth more esteem it than the very nature of the thing deserveth. And then who doth not plainly see how far it is under iron, as without the which men can no better live than without fire and water. Whereas to gold and silver nature hath given no use that we may not well lack, if that the folly of men had not set it in higher estimation for the rareness' sake. But of the contrary part, nature as a most tender and loving mother, hath placed the best and most necessary things open abroad; as the air, the water, and the earth itself; and hath removed and hid farthest from us vain and unprofitable things. Therefore if these metals among them should be fast locked up in some tower, it might be suspected that the prince and the council (as the people is ever foolishly imagining) intended by some subtlety to deceive the commons, and to take some profit of it to themselves. Furthermore if they should make thereof plate and such other finely and cunningly wrought stuff, if at any time they should have occasion to break it and melt it again, therewith to pay their soldiers' wages, they see and perceive very well that men would be loath to part from those things that they once began to have pleasure and delight in.

To remedy all this they have found out a means, which, as it is agreeable to all their other laws and customs, so it is from ours, where gold is so much set by, and so diligently kept, very far discrepant and repugnant; and therefore incredible, but only to them that be wise. For whereas they eat and drink in earthen and glass vessels, which indeed be curiously and properly made, and yet be of very small value, of gold and silver they make commonly chamber-pots, and other vessels that serve for most vile uses, not only in their common halls, but in every man's private house. Furthermore of the same metals they make great chains, fetters, and gyves wherein they tie their bondmen. Finally, whosoever for any offence be infamed, by their ears hang rings of gold; upon their fingers they wear rings of gold, and about their necks chains of gold; and in conclusion their heads be tied about with gold. Thus by all means possible they procure to have gold and silver among them in reproach and infamy. And these metals, which other nations do as grievously and sorrowfully forego, as in a manner their own lives, if they should altogether at once be taken from the Utopians, no man there would think that he had lost the worth of one farthing.

They gather also pearls by the seaside, and diamonds and carbuncles upon certain rocks; and yet they seek not for them, but by chance finding them, they cut and polish them. And therewith they deck their young infants. Which like as in the first years of their childhood, they make much and be fond and proud of such ornaments, so when they be a little more grown in years and discretion, perceiving that none but children do wear such toys and trifles, they lay them away even of their own shamefastness, without any bidding of their parents: even as our children, when they wax big, do cast away nuts, brooches, and puppets. Therefore these laws and customs, which be so far different from all other nations, how diverse fantasies also and minds they do cause, did I never so plainly perceive, as in the ambassadors of the Anemolians.

These ambassadors came to Amaurote while I was there. And because they came to entreat of great and weighty matters, those three citizens apiece out of every city were come thither before them. But all the ambassadors of the next countries, which had been there before, and knew the fashions and manners of the Utopians, among whom they perceived no honour given to sumptuous apparel, silks to be contemned, gold also to be infamed and reproachful, were wont to come thither in very homely and simple array. But the Anemolians, because they dwell far thence and had very little acquaintance with them, hearing that they were all apparelled alike, and that very rudely and homely; thinking them not to have the things which they did not wear; being, therefore, more proud than wise; determined in the gorgeousness of their apparel to represent very gods, and with the bright shining and glistering of their gay clothing to dazzle the eyes of the silly poor Utopians. So there came in three ambassadors with a hundred servants all apparelled in changeable colours; the most of them in silks, the ambassadors themselves (for at home in their own country they were noble men) in cloth of gold, with great chains of gold, with gold hanging at their ears, with gold rings upon their fingers, with brooches and aglets of gold upon their caps, which glistered full of pearls and precious stones: to be short, trimmed and adorned with all those things, which among the Utopians were either the punishment of bondmen, of the reproach of infamed persons, or else trifles for young children to play withal. Therefore it would have done a man good at his heart to have seen how proudly they displayed their peacocks' feathers, how much they made of their painted sheaths, and how lofty they set forth and advanced themselves, when they compared their gallant apparel with the poor raiment of the Utopians. For all the people were swarmed forth into the streets. And on the other side it was no less pleasure to consider how much they were deceived, and how far they missed of their purpose, being contrariwise taken than they thought they should have been. For to the eyes of all the Utopians, except very few, which had been in other countries for some reasonable cause, all that gorgeousness of apparel seemed shameful and reproachful. Insomuch that they most reverently saluted the vilest and most abject of them for lords: passing over the ambassadors themselves without any

honour: judging them by their wearing of golden chains to be
bondmen. Yea, you should have seen children also, that had cast
away their pearls and precious stones, when they saw the like sticking
upon the ambassadors' caps, dig and push their mothers under the
sides, saying thus to them: 'Look, mother, how great a lubber doth
yet wear pearls and precious stones, as though he were a little child
still.' But the mother, yea and that also in good earnest: 'Peace, son,'
saith she: 'I think he be some of the ambassadors' fools.' Some found
fault at their golden chains, as to no use nor purpose, being so small
and weak that a bondman might easily break them, and again so wide
and large that when it pleased him he might cast them off, and run
away at liberty whither he would.

But when the ambassadors had been there a day or two and saw so
great abundance of gold so lightly esteemed, yea, in no less reproach
than it was with them in honour; and besides that more gold in the
chains and gyves of one fugitive bondman than all the costly
ornaments of them three were worth; they began to abate their
courage, and for very shame laid away all that gorgeous array whereof
they were so proud, and especially when they had talked familiarly
with the Utopians, and had learned all their fashions and opinions.
For they marvel that any men be so foolish as to have delight and
pleasure in the doubtful glistering of a little trifling stone, which may
behold any of the stars, or else the sun itself. Or that any man is so
mad as to count himself the nobler for the smaller or finer thread of
wool, which selfsame wool (be it now in never so fine a spun thread)
a sheep did once wear; and yet was she all that time no other thing
than a sheep.

They marvel also that gold, which of the own nature is a thing so
unprofitable, is now among all people in so high estimation, that man
himself, by whom, yea, and for the use of whom, it is so much set by,
is in much less estimation than the gold itself. Insomuch that a
lumpish, block-headed churl, and which hath no more wit than an
ass, yea, and as full of naughtiness as of folly, shall have nevertheless
many wise and good men in subjection and bondage, only for this,
because he hath a great heap of gold. Which if it should be taken
from him by any fortune, or by some subtle wile and cautel of the
law (which no less than fortune doth both raise up the low and pluck
down the high), and be given to the most vile slave and abject drivel
of all his household, then shortly after he shall go into the service of

his servant as an augmentation or overplus beside his money. But
they much more marvel at and detest the madness of them, which to
those rich men, in whose debt and danger they be not, do give almost
divine honours, for none other consideration but because they be
rich; and yet knowing them to be such niggardish penny-fathers, that
they be sure as long as, they live, not the worth of one farthing of that
heap of gold shall come to them.

These and suchlike opinions have they conceived, partly by
education, being brought up in that commonwealth whose laws and
customs be far different from these kinds of folly, and partly by good
literature and learning. For though there be not many in every city
which be exempt and discharged of all other labours, and appointed
only to learning, that is to say, such in whom even from their very
childhood they have perceived a singular towardness, a fine wit, and a
mind apt to good learning; yet all in their childhood be instructed in
learning. And the better part of the people, both men and women,
throughout all their whole life do bestow on learning those spare
hours which we said they have vacant from bodily labours. They be
taught learning in their own native tongue. For it is both copious in
words, and also pleasant to the ear; and for the utterance of a man's
mind very perfect and sure. The most part of all that side of the world
useth the same language, saving that among the Utopians it is finest
and purest, and according to the diversity of the countries it is
diversely altered.

Of all these philosophers whose names be here famous in this part
of the world to us known, before our coming thither not as much as
the fame of any of them was come among them. And yet in music,
logic, arithmetic, and geometry they have found out in a manner all
that our ancient philosophers have taught. But as they in all things be
almost equal to our old ancient clerks, so our new logicians in subtle
inventions have far passed and gone beyond them. For they have not
devised one of all those rules of restrictions, amplifications, and
suppositions, very wittily invented in the small logicals, which here
our children in every place do learn. Furthermore they were never
yet able to find out the second intentions; insomuch that none of
them all could ever see man himself in common, as they call him,
though he be (as you know) bigger than ever was any giant, yea, and
pointed to of us even with our finger.

But they be in the course of the stars and the movings of the heavenly spheres very expert and cunning. They have also wittily excogitated and devised instruments of divers fashions, wherein is exactly comprehended and contained the movings and situations of the sun, the moon, and of all the other stars, which appear in their horizon. But as for the amities and dissensions of the planets, and all that deceitful divination by the stars, they never as much as dreamed thereof. Rains, winds, and other courses of tempests they know before by certain tokens, which they have learned by long use and observation. But of the causes of all these things, and of the ebbing, flowing, and saltness of the sea, and, finally, of the original beginning and nature of heaven and of the world, they hold partly the same opinions that our old philosophers hold, and partly, as our philosophers vary among themselves, so they also, while they bring new reasons of things, do disagree from all them, and yet among themselves in all points they do not accord.

In that part of philosophy which entreateth of manners and virtue, their reasons and opinions agree with ours. They dispute of the good qualities of the soul, of the body, and of fortune; and whether the name of goodness may be applied to all these, or only to the endowments and gifts of the soul. They reason of virtue and pleasure. But the chief and principal question is in what thing, be it one or more, the felicity of man consisteth. But in this point they seem almost too much given and inclined to the opinion of them which defend pleasure, wherein they determine either all or the chiefest part of man's felicity to rest. And (which is more to be marvelled at) the defence of this so dainty and delicate an opinion they fetch even from their grave, sharp, bitter, and rigorous religion. For they never dispute of felicity or blessedness, but they join unto the reasons of philosophy certain principles taken out of religion; without the which to the investigation of true felicity they think reason of itself weak and imperfect.

Those principles be these and suchlike. That the soul is immortal, and by the bountiful goodness of God ordained to felicity. That to our virtues and good deeds rewards be appointed after this life, and to our evil deeds punishments. Though these be pertaining to religion, yet they think it meet that they should be believed and granted by proofs of reason. But if these principles were condemned and disannulled, then without any delay they pronounce no man to be so foolish, which would not do all his diligence and endeavour to obtain pleasure by right or wrong, only avoiding this inconvenience, that the less pleasure should not be a let or hindrance to the bigger; or that he laboured not for that pleasure which would bring after it displeasure, grief, and sorrow. For they judge it extreme madness to follow sharp and painful virtue, and not only to banish the pleasure of life, but also willingly to suffer grief, without any hope of profit thereof ensuing. For what profit can there be, if a man, when he hath passed over all his life unpleasantly, that is to say, miserably, shall have no reward after his death?

But now, sir, they think not felicity to rest in all pleasure, but only in that pleasure that is good and honest, and that hereto, as to perfect blessedness, our nature is allured and drawn even of virtue, whereto only they that be of the contrary opinion do attribute felicity. For they define virtue to be life ordered according to nature, and that we be hereunto ordained of God. And that he doth follow the course of nature, which in desiring and refusing things is ruled by reason.

Furthermore that reason doth chiefly and principally kindle in men the love and veneration of the divine Majesty. Of whose goodness it is that we be, and that we be in possibility to attain felicity. And that secondarily it both stirreth and provoketh us to lead our life out of care in joy and mirth, and also moveth us to help and further all other in respect of the society of nature to obtain and enjoy the same. For there was never man so earnest and painful a follower of virtue and hater of pleasure, that would so enjoin your labours, watchings, and fastings, but he would also exhort you to ease, lighten, and relieve, to your power, the lack and misery of others, praising the same as a deed of humanity and pity. Then if it be a point of humanity for man to bring health and comfort to man, and specially (which is a virtue most peculiarly belonging to man) to mitigate and assuage the grief of others, and by taking from them the sorrow and heaviness of life, to restore them to joy, that is to say to pleasure; why may it not then be said that nature doth provoke every man to do the same to himself? For a joyful life, that is to say, a pleasant life is either evil; and if it be so, then thou shouldest not only help no man thereto, but rather, as much as in thee lieth, withdraw all men from it, as noisome and hurtful; or else if thou not only mayest, but also of duty art bound to procure it to others, why not chiefly to thyself? To whom thou art bound to show as much favour and gentleness as to others. For when nature biddeth thee to be good and gentle to others she commandeth thee not to be cruel and ungentle to thyself.

Therefore even very nature (say they) prescribeth to us a joyful life, that is to say, pleasure as the end of all our operations. And they define virtue to be life ordered according to the prescript of nature. But in that that nature doth allure and provoke men one to help another to live merrily (which surely she doth not without a good cause: for no man is so far above the lot of man's state or condition, that nature doth cark and care for him only, which equally favoureth all that be comprehended under the communion of one shape, form, and fashion), verily she commandeth thee to use diligent circumspection, that thou do not so seek for thine own commodities that thou procure others' incommodities.

Wherefore their opinion is, that not only covenants and bargains made among private men ought to be well and faithfully fulfilled, observed, and kept, but also common laws, which either a good prince hath justly published, or else the people neither oppressed with tyranny, neither deceived by fraud and guile, hath by their common consent constituted and ratified, concerning the partition of the commodities of life, that is to say, the matter of pleasure. These laws not offended, it is wisdom that thou look to thine own wealth. And to do the same for the commonwealth is no less than thy duty, if thou bearest any reverent love, or any natural zeal and affection to thy native country. But to go about to let another man of his pleasure, whilst thou procurest thine own, that is open wrong.

Contrariwise to withdraw something from thyself to give to others, that is a point of humanity and gentleness; which never taketh away so much commodity as it bringeth again. For it is recompensed with the return of benefits, and the conscience of the good deed, with the remembrance of the thankful love and benevolence of them to whom thou hast done it, doth bring more pleasure to thy mind, than that which thou hast withholden from thyself could have brought to thy body. Finally (which to a godly disposed and a religious mind is easy to be persuaded), God recompenseth the gift of a short and small pleasure with great and everlasting joy. Therefore, the matter diligently weighed and considered, thus they think that all our actions, and in them the virtues themselves be referred at the last to pleasure, as their end and felicity.

Pleasure they call every motion and state of the body or mind, wherein man hath naturally delectation. Appetite they join to nature, and that not without a good cause. For like as, not only the senses, but also right reason coveteth whatsoever is naturally pleasant, so that it may be gotten without wrong or injury, not letting or debarring a greater pleasure, nor causing painful labour, even so those things that men by vain imagination do feign against nature to be pleasant (as though it lay in their power to change the things, as they do the names of things), all such pleasures they believe to be of so small help and furtherance to felicity, that they count them a great let and hindrance, because that, in whom they have once taken place, all his mind they possess with a false opinion of pleasure. So that there is no place left for true and natural delectations. For there be many things which of their own nature contain no pleasantness; yea, the most part of them much grief and sorrow. And yet through the perverse and malicious flickering enticements of lewd and unhonest desires be taken not only for special and sovereign pleasures, but also be counted among the chief causes of life.

In this counterfeit kind of pleasure they put them that I spake of before. Which the better gowns they have on, the better men they think themselves. In the which thing they do twice err. For they be no less deceived in that they think their gown the better, than they be in that they think themselves the better. For if you consider the profitable use of the garment, why should wool of a finer spun thread be thought better than the wool of a coarse spun thread? Yet they, as though the one did pass the other by nature, and not by their mistaking, advance themselves, and think the price of their own persons thereby greatly increased. And therefore the honour, which in a coarse gown they durst not have looked for, they require, as it were of duty, for their finer gown's sake. And if they be passed by without reverence, they take it displeasantly and disdainfully.

And again is it not like madness to take a pride in vain and unprofitable honours? For what natural or true pleasure dost thou take of another man's bare head or bowed knees? Will this ease the pain of thy knees, or remedy the frenzy of thy head? In this image of counterfeit pleasure, they be of a marvellous madness, which for the opinion of nobility, rejoice much in their own conceit. Because it was their fortune to come of such ancestors, whose stock of long time hath been counted rich (for now nobility is nothing else), specially rich in lands. And though their ancestors left them not one foot of land, or else they themselves have pissed it against the walls, yet they think themselves not the less noble therefore of one hair.

In this number also they count them that take pleasure and delight (as I said) in gems and precious stones, and think themselves almost gods, if they chance to get an excellent one, specially of that kind which in that time of their own countrymen is had in highest estimation. For one kind of stone keepeth not his price still in all countries and at all times. Nor they buy them not, but taken out of the gold and bare: no nor so neither, until they have made the seller to swear that he will warrant and assure it to be a true stone, and no counterfeit gem. Such care they take lest a counterfeit stone should deceive their eyes instead of a right stone. But why shouldest thou not take even as much pleasure in beholding a counterfeit stone which thine eye cannot discern from a right stone? They should both be of like value to thee, even as to the blind man.

What shall I say of them that keep superfluous riches, to take delectation only in the beholding, and not in the use or occupying thereof? Do they take true pleasure, or else be they deceived with false pleasure? Or of them that be in a contrary vice, hiding the gold which they shall never occupy, nor peradventure never see more? And whilst they take care lest they shall lose it, do lose it indeed. For what is it else, when they hide it in the ground, taking it both from their own use, and perchance from all other men's also? And yet thou, when thou hast hid thy treasure, as one out of all care, hoppest for joy. The which treasure, if it should chance to be stolen, and thou, ignorant of the theft, shouldest die ten years after: all that ten years' space that thou livedst after thy money was stolen, what matter was it to thee whether it had been taken away or else safe as thou leftest it? Truly both ways like profit came to thee.

To these so foolish pleasures they join dicers, whose madness they know by hearsay, and not by use. Hunters also, and hawkers. For what pleasure is there (say they) in casting the dice upon a table. Which thou hast done so often, that if there were any pleasure in it, yet the oft use might make thee weary thereof? Or what delight can there be, and not rather displeasure in hearing the barking and howling of dogs? Or what greater pleasure is there to be felt, when a dog followeth a hare, than when a dog followeth a dog? For one thing is done in both, that is to say, running, if thou hast pleasure therein. But if the hope of slaughter and the expectation of tearing in pieces the beast doth please thee, thou shouldest rather be moved with pity to see a silly, innocent hare murdered of a dog, the weak of the stronger, the fearful of the fierce, the innocent of the cruel and unmerciful. Therefore all this exercise of hunting, as a thing unworthy to be used of free men, the Utopians have rejected to their butchers, to the which craft (as we said before) they appoint their bondsmen. For they count hunting the lowest, the vilest, and most abject part of butchery, and the other parts of it more profitable, and more honest, as bringing much more commodity, in that they kill beasts only for necessity. Whereas the hunter seeketh nothing but pleasure of the silly and woeful beasts' slaughter and murder. The which pleasure in beholding death they think doth rise in the very beasts, either of a cruel affection of mind, or else to be changed in continuance of time into cruelty, by long use of so cruel a pleasure.

These therefore and all such like, which be innumerable, though the common sort of people doth take them for pleasures, yet they, seeing there is no natural pleasantness in them, do plainly determine them to have no affinity with true and right pleasure. For as touching that they do commonly move the sense with delectation (which seemeth to be a work of pleasure) this doth nothing diminish their opinion. For not the nature of the thing, but their perverse and lewd custom is the cause hereof. Which causeth them to accept bitter or sour things for sweet things. Even as women with child in their vitiate and corrupt taste, think pitch and tallow sweeter than any honey. Howbeit no man's judgment depraved and corrupt, either by sickness or by custom, can change the nature of pleasure, more than it can do the nature of other things.

They make divers kinds of pleasures. For some they attribute to the soul, and some to the body. To the soul they give intelligence, and that delectation that cometh of the contemplation of truth. Hereunto is joined the pleasant remembrance of the good life past.*

The pleasure of the body they divide into two parts. The first is when delectation is sensibly felt and perceived. Which many times chanceth by the renewing and refreshing of those parts which our natural heat drieth up. This cometh by meat and drink. And sometimes while those things be expulsed, and voided, whereof is in the body over great abundance. This pleasure is felt when we do our natural easement, or when we be doing the act of generation, or when the itching of any part is eased with rubbing or scratching. Sometimes

* Robinson omits the phrase that follows, 'and the sure hope of future happiness.'

pleasure riseth, exhibiting to any member nothing that it desireth, nor taking from it any pain that it feeleth, which nevertheless tickleth and moveth our senses with a certain secret efficacy, but with a manifest motion turneth them to it, as is that which cometh of music.

The second part of bodily pleasure, they say, is that which consisteth and resteth in the quiet and upright state of the body. And that truly is every man's own proper health intermingled and disturbed with no grief. For this, if it be not letted nor assaulted with no grief, is delectable of itself, though it be moved with no external or outward pleasure. For though it be not so plain and manifest to the sense as the greedy lust of eating and drinking, yet nevertheless many take it for the chiefest pleasure. All the Utopians grant it to be a right sovereign pleasure, and as you would say the foundation and ground of all pleasures, as which even alone is able to make the state and condition of life delectable and pleasant. And it being once taken away, there is no place left for any pleasure. For to be without grief not having health, that they call unsensibility, and not pleasure.

The Utopians have long ago rejected and condemned the opinion of them which said that steadfast and quiet health (for this question also hath been diligently debated among them) ought not therefore to be counted a pleasure, because they say it cannot be presently and sensibly perceived and felt by some outward motion. But of the contrary part now they agree almost all in this, that health is a most sovereign pleasure. For seeing that in sickness (say they) is grief, which is a mortal enemy to pleasure, even as sickness is to health, why should not then pleasure be in the quietness of health? For they say it maketh nothing to this matter, whether you say that sickness is a grief, or that in sickness is grief, for all cometh to one purpose. For whether health be a pleasure itself, or a necessary cause of pleasure, as fire is of heat, truly both ways it followeth, that they cannot be without pleasure that be in perfect health. Furthermore, whilst we eat (say they) then health, which began to be appaired, fighteth by the help of food against hunger. In the which fight, whilst health by little and little getteth the upper hand, that same proceeding, and (as you would say) that onwardness to the wonted strength ministereth that pleasure whereby we be so refreshed. Health, therefore, which in the conflict is joyful, shall it not be merry when it hath got the victory? But as soon as it hath recovered the pristinate strength, which thing only in all the fight it coveted, shall it incontinent be astonied? Nor

shall it not know nor embrace the own wealth and goodness? For
where it is said, health cannot be felt; this, they think, is nothing true.
For what man waking, say they, feeleth not himself in health, but he
that is not? Is there any man so possessed with stonish insensibility, or
with lethargy, that is to say, the sleeping sickness, that he will not
grant health to be acceptable to him and delectable? But what other
thing is delectation than that which by another name is called
pleasure?

They embrace chiefly the pleasures of the mind. For them they
count the chiefest and most principal of all. The chief part of them
they think doth come of the exercise of virtue, and conscience of
good life. Of these pleasures that the body ministereth, they give the
pre-eminence to health. For the delight of eating and drinking, and
whatsoever hath any like pleasantness, they determine to be pleasures
much to be desired, but no other ways than for health's sake. For
such things of their own proper nature be not so pleasant, but in that
they resist sickness privily stealing on. Therefore like as it is a wise
man's part, rather to avoid sickness than to wish for medicines, and
rather to drive away and put to flight careful griefs than to call for
comfort; so it is much better not to need this kind of pleasure than
thereby to be eased of the contrary grief. The which kind of pleasure,
if any man take for his felicity, that man must needs grant, that then
he shall be in most felicity, if he live that life which is led in continual
hunger, thirst, itching, eating, drinking, scratching, and rubbing. The
which life how not only foul and unhonest, but also how miserable
and wretched it is, who perceiveth not? These doubtless be the basest
pleasures of all, as unpure and unperfect. For they never come, but
accompanied with their contrary griefs. As with the pleasure of eating
is joined hunger, and that after no very equal sort. For of these two
the grief is both the more vehement, and also of longer continuance.
For it beginneth before the pleasure, and endeth not until the
pleasure die with it.

Wherefore such pleasures they think not greatly to be set by, but in
that they be necessary. Howbeit they have delight also in these, and
thankfully knowledge the tender love of mother nature, which with
most pleasant delectation allureth her children to that, to the
necessary use whereof they must from time to time continually be
forced and driven. For how wretched and miserable should our life
be, if these daily griefs of hunger and thirst could not be driven away,

but with bitter potions and sour medicines, as the other diseases be, wherewith we be seldomer troubled?

But beauty, strength, nimbleness, these as peculiar and pleasant gifts of nature they make much of. But those pleasures that be received by the ears, the eyes, and the nose, which nature willeth to be proper and peculiar to man (for no other living creature doth behold the fairness and the beauty of the world, or is moved with any respect of savours, but only for the diversity of meats, neither perceiveth the concordant and discordant distances of sounds and tunes), these pleasures, I say, they accept and allow as certain pleasant rejoicings of life.

But in all things this cautel they use, that a less pleasure hinder not a bigger, and that the pleasure be no cause of displeasure, which they think to follow of necessity, if the pleasure be unhonest. But yet to despise the comeliness of beauty, to waste the bodily strength, to turn nimbleness into sluggishness, to consume and make feeble the body with fasting, to do injury to health, and to reject the pleasant motions of nature; unless a man neglect these commodities, whiles he doth with a fervent zeal procure the wealth of others, or the common profit, for the which pleasure forborne, he is in hope of a greater pleasure at God's hand; else for a vain shadow of virtue, for the wealth and profit of no man, to punish himself, or to the intent he may be able courageously to suffer adversity, which perchance shall never come to him, this to do they think it a point of extreme madness, and a token of a man cruelly minded towards himself, and unkind towards nature, as one so disdaining to be in her danger that he renounceth and refuseth all her benefits.

This is their sentence and opinion of virtue and pleasure. And they believe that by man's reason none can be found truer than this, unless any godlier be inspired into man from heaven. Wherein whether they believe well or no, neither the time doth suffer us to discuss, neither it is now necessary. For we have taken upon us to show and declare their laws and ordinances, and not to defend them.

But this thing I believe verily: howsoever these decrees be, that there is in no place of the world, neither a more excellent people, neither a more flourishing commonwealth. They be light and quick of body, full of activity and nimbleness, and of more strength than a man would judge them by their stature, which, for all that, is not too low. And though their soil be not very fruitful, nor their air very wholesome, yet against the air they so defend them with temperate diet, and so order and husband their ground with diligent travail, that in no country is greater increase and plenty of corn and cattle, nor men's bodies of longer life, and subject or apt to fewer diseases.

There, therefore, a man may see well and diligently exploited and furnished, not only those things which husbandmen do commonly in other countries, as by craft and cunning to remedy the barrenness of the ground; but also a whole wood by the hands of the people plucked up by the roots in one place, and set again in another place. Wherein was had regard and consideration, not of plenty, but of commodious carriage, that wood and timber might be nigher to the sea, or the rivers, or the cities. For it is less labour and business to carry grain far by land, than wood. The people be gentle, merry, quick, and fine-witted, delighting in quietness, and when need requireth, able to abide and suffer much bodily labour. Else they be not greatly desirous and fond of it; but in the exercise and study of the mind they be never weary.

When they had heard me speak of the Greek literature or learning (for in Latin, there was nothing that I thought they would greatly allow, besides historians and poets) they made wonderful, earnest, and importunate suit unto me that I would teach and instruct them in that tongue and learning. I began, therefore, to read unto them, at the first truly more because I would not seem to refuse the labour, than that I hoped that they would anything profit therein. But when I had gone forward a little, I perceived incontinent by their diligence, that my labour should not be bestowed in vain. For they began so easily to fashion their letters, so plainly to pronounce the words, so quickly to learn by heart, and so surely to rehearse the same, that I marvelled at it, saving that the most part of them were fine and chosen wits, and of ripe age, picked out of the company of the learned men, which not only of their own free and voluntary will, but also by the commandment of the council, undertook to learn this language. Therefore in less than three years' space there was nothing in the Greek tongue that they lacked. They were able to read good authors without any stay, if the book were not false.

This kind of learning, as I suppose, they took so much the sooner, because it is somewhat alliant to them. For I think that this nation took their beginning of the Greeks, because their speech, which in all other points is not much unlike the Persian tongue, keepeth divers signs and tokens of the Greek language in the names of their cities and of their magistrates.

They have of me (for when I was determined to enter into my fourth voyage, I cast into the ship in the stead of merchandise a pretty fardel of books, because I intended to come again rather never than shortly), they have, I say, of me the most part of Plato's works, more of Aristotle's, also Theophrastus of plants, but in divers places (which I am sorry for) imperfect. For whilst we were aship board, a marmoset chanced upon the book, as it was negligently laid by, which, wantonly playing therewith, plucked out certain leaves, and tore them in pieces. Of them that have written the grammar, they have only Lascaris. For Theodorus I carried not with me, nor never a dictionary, but Hesychius, and Dioscorides. They set great store by Plutarch's books. And they be delighted with Lucian's merry conceits and jests. Of the poets they have Aristophanes, Homer, Euripides, and Sophocles in Aldus' small print. Of the historians they have Thucydides, Herodotus, and Herodian. Also my companion, Tricius Apinatus, carried with him physic books, certain small works of Hippocrates, and Galenus' *Microtechne*. The which book they have in great estimation.

For though there be almost no nation under heaven that hath less need of physic than they, yet this notwithstanding, physic is nowhere in greater honour. Because they count the knowledge of it among the goodliest and most profitable parts of philosophy. For whilst they by the help of this philosophy search out the secret mysteries of nature, they think themselves to receive thereby not only wonderful great pleasure, but also to obtain great thanks and favour of the author and maker thereof. Whom they think, according to the fashion of other artificers, to have set forth the marvellous and gorgeous frame of the world for man with great affection intentively to behold, whom only he hath made of wit and capacity to consider and understand the excellency of so great a work. And therefore he beareth (say they) more goodwill and love to the curious and diligent beholder and viewer of his work, and marveller at the same, than he doth to him, which like a very brute beast, without wit and reason, or as one without sense or moving, hath no regard to so great and so wonderful a spectacle.

The wits, therefore, of the Utopians, inured and exercised in learning, be marvellous quick in the invention of feats helping anything to the advantage and wealth of life. Howbeit two feats they may thank us for. That is the science of imprinting, and the craft of making paper. And yet not only us, but chiefly and principally themselves.

For when we showed to them Aldus' print in books of paper, and told them of the stuff whereof paper is made, and of the feat of graving letters, speaking somewhat more than we could plainly declare (for there was none of us that knew perfectly either the one or the other), they forthwith very wittily conjectured the thing. And whereas before they wrote only in skins, in barks of trees, and in reeds, now they have attempted to make paper, and to imprint letters. And though at the first it proved not all of the best, yet, by often assaying the same, they shortly got the feat of both. And have so brought the matter about, that if they had copies of Greek authors, they could lack no books. But now they have no more than I rehearsed before, saving that by printing of books they have multiplied and increased the same into many thousands of copies.

Whosoever cometh thither to see the land, being excellent in any gift of wit, or through much and long journeying well experienced and seen in the knowledge of many countries (for the which cause we were very welcome to them), him they receive and entertain wondrous gently and lovingly. For they have delight to hear what is done in every land, howbeit very few merchantmen come thither. For what should they bring thither, unless it were iron, or else gold and silver, which they had rather carry home again? Also such things as are to be carried out of their land, they think it more wisdom to carry that gear forth themselves, than that others should come thither to fetch it, to the intent they may the better know the outlands on every side of them, and keep in ure the feat and knowledge of sailing.

Of Bondmen, Sick Persons, Wedlock, and divers other Matters

They neither make bondmen of prisoners taken in battle, unless it be in battle that they fought themselves, nor of bondmen's children, nor, to be short, of any such as they can get out of foreign countries, though he were there a bondman. But either such as among themselves for heinous offences be punished with bondage, or else such as in the cities of other lands for great trespasses be condemned to death. And of this sort of bondmen they have most store. For many of them they bring home, sometimes paying very little for them, yea, most commonly getting them for gramercy. These sorts of bondmen they keep not only in continual work and labour, but also in bands. But their own men they handle hardest, whom they judge more desperate, and to have deserved greater punishment, because they being so godly brought up to virtue in so excellent a commonwealth, could not for all that be refrained from misdoing.

Another kind of bondman they have, when a vile drudge being a poor labourer in another country doth choose of his own free will to be a bondman among them. These they entreat and order honestly, and entertain almost as gently as their own free citizens, saving that they put them to a little more labour, as thereto accustomed. If any such be disposed to depart thence (which seldom is seen), they neither hold him against his will, neither send him away with empty hands.

The sick (as I said) they see to with great affection, and let nothing at all pass concerning either physic or good diet, whereby they may be restored again to their health. Such as be sick of incurable diseases they comfort with sitting by them, with talking with them, and, to be short, with all manner of helps that may be. But if the disease be not only incurable, but also full of continual pain and anguish, then the priests and the magistrates exhort the man, seeing he is not able to do any

duty of life, and by overliving his own death is noisome and irksome
to others, and grievous to himself, that he will determine with himself
no longer to cherish that pestilent and painful disease. And seeing his
life is to him but a torment, that he will not be unwilling to die, but
rather take a good hope to him, and either despatch himself out of that
painful life, as out of a prison, or a rack of torment, or else suffer
himself willingly to be rid out of it by others. And in so doing they tell
him he shall do wisely, seeing by his death he shall lose no commodity,
but end his pain. And because in that act he shall follow the counsel of
the priests, that is to say, of the interpreters of God's will and pleasure,
they show him that he shall do like a godly and a virtuous man.

They that be thus persuaded, finish their lives willingly, either with
hunger, or else die in their sleep without any feeling of death. But
they cause none such to die against his will, nor they use no less
diligence and attendance about him, believing this to be an honourable death. Else he that killeth himself before that the priests and the
counsel have allowed the cause of his death, him as unworthy either
to be buried, or with fire to be consumed, they cast unburied into
some stinking marsh.

The woman is not married before she be eighteen years old. The
man is four years older before he marry. If either the man or the
woman be proved to have actually offended before their marriage,
with another, the party that so hath trespassed is sharply punished.
And both the offenders be forbidden ever after in all their life to
marry, unless the fault be forgiven by the prince's pardon. But both
the goodman and the goodwife of the house where that offence was
committed, as being slack and negligent in looking to their charge, be
in danger of great reproach and infamy. That offence is so sharply
punished, because they perceive, that unless they be diligently kept
from the liberty of this vice, few will join together in the love of
marriage, wherein all the life must be led with one, and also all the
griefs and displeasures coming therewith patiently be taken and borne.

Furthermore in choosing wives and husbands they observe earnestly and straightly a custom which seemed to us very fond and
foolish. For a sad and honest matron showeth the woman, be she
maid or widow, naked to the wooer. And likewise a sage and discreet
man exhibiteth the wooer naked to the woman. At this custom we
laughed, and disallowed it as foolish.

But they on the other part do greatly wonder at the folly of all other

nations, which in buying a colt, whereas a little money is in hazard, be
so chary and circumspect, that though he be almost all bare, yet they
will not buy him, unless the saddle and all the harness be taken off, lest
under those coverings be hid some gall or sore. And yet in choosing a
wife, which shall be either pleasure or displeasure to them all their life
after, they be so reckless, that all the residue of the woman's body
being covered with clothes, they esteem her scarcely by one handbreath
(for they can see no more but her face), and so to join her to them not
without great jeopardy of evil agreeing together, if anything in her
body afterward should chance to offend and mislike them. For all men
be not so wise as to have respect to the virtuous conditions of the
party. And the endowments of the body cause the virtues of the mind
more to be esteemed and regarded, yea, even in the marriages of wise
men. Verily so foul deformity may be hid under those coverings, that
it may quite alienate and take away the man's mind from his wife,
when it shall not be lawful for their bodies to be separate again. If such
deformity happen by any chance after the marriage is consummate and
finished, well, there is no remedy but patience. Every man must take
his fortune well a worth. But it were well done that a law were made
whereby all such deceits might be eschewed and avoided beforehand.

And this were they constrained more earnestly to look upon,
because they only of the nations in that part of the world be content
every man with one wife apiece. And matrimony is there never
broken, but by death; except adultery break the bond, or else the
intolerable wayward manners of either party. For if either of them
find themselves for any such cause grieved, they may by the licence of
the council change and take another. But the other party liveth ever
after in infamy and out of wedlock. Howbeit the husband to put
away his wife for no other fault, but for that some mishap is fallen to
her body, this by no means they will suffer. For they judge it a great
point of cruelty, that anybody in their most need of help and comfort
should be cast off and forsaken, and that old age, which both bringeth
sickness with it, and is a sickness itself, should unkindly and
unfaithfully be dealt withal.

But now and then it chanceth, whereas the man and the woman
cannot well agree between themselves, both of them finding other
with whom they hope to live more quietly and merrily, that they by
the full consent of them both be divorced asunder and married again
to other. But that not without the authority of the council. Which

agreeth to no divorces before they and their wives have diligently tried and examined the matter. Yea, and then also they be loth to consent to it, because they know this to be the next way to break love between man and wife, to be in easy hope of a new marriage.

Breakers of wedlock be punished with most grievous bondage. And if both the offenders were married, then the parties which in that behalf have suffered wrong, being divorced from the advoutrers, be married together, if they will, or else to whom they lust. But if either of them both do still continue in love toward so unkind a bedfellow, the use of wedlock is not to them forbidden, if the party faultless be disposed to follow in toiling and drudgery the person which for that offence is condemned to bondage. And very oft it chanceth that the repentance of the one, and the earnest diligence of the other, doth so move the prince with pity and compassion, that he restoreth the bond person from servitude to liberty and freedom again. But if the same party be taken eftsoons in that fault, there is no other way but death.

To other trespasses no prescript punishment is appointed by any law. But according to the heinousness of the offence, or contrary, so the punishment is moderated by the discretion of the council. The husbands chastise their wives, and the parents their children, unless they have done any so horrible an offence that the open punishment thereof maketh much for the advancement of honest manners. But most commonly the most heinous faults be punished with the incommodity of bondage. For that they suppose to be to the offenders no less grief, and to the commonwealth more profit, than if they should hastily put them to death, and so make them quite out of the way. For there cometh more profit of their labour than of their death, and by their example they fear other the longer from like offences. But if they being thus used, do rebel and kick again, then forsooth they be slain as desperate and wild beasts, whom neither prison nor chain could restrain and keep under. But they which take their bondage patiently be not left all hopeless. For after they have been broken and tamed with long miseries, if then they show such repentance, as thereby it may be perceived that they be sorrier for their offence than for their punishment, sometimes by the prince's prerogative, and sometimes by the voice and consent of the people, their bondage either is mitigated, or else clean released and forgiven. He that moveth to advoutry is in no less danger and jeopardy than if he had committed advoutry in deed. For in all offences they count the intent and pretensed purpose as evil as the act or deed itself, thinking that no let ought to excuse him that did his best to have no let.

They have singular delight and pleasure in fools. And as it is a great reproach to do any of them hurt or injury, so they prohibit not to take pleasure of foolishness. For that, they think, doth much good to the fools. And if any man be so sad and stern, that he cannot laugh neither at their words, nor at their deeds, none of them be committed to his tuition, for fear lest he would not entreat them gently and favourably enough; to whom they should bring no delectation (for other goodness in them is none), much less any profit should they yield him.

To mock a man for his deformity, or for that he lacketh any part or limb of his body, is counted great dishonesty and reproach, not to him that is mocked, but to him that mocketh. Which unwisely doth upbraid any man of that as a vice, that was not in his power to eschew. Also as they count and reckon very little wit to be in him that regardeth not natural beauty and comeliness, so to help the same with paintings is taken for a vain and a wanton pride, not without great infamy. For they know even by very experience that no comeliness of beauty doth so highly commend and advance the wives in the conceit of their husbands, as honest conditions and lowliness. For as love is oftentimes won with beauty, so it is not kept, preserved, and continued but by virtue and obedience.

They do not only fear their people from doing evil by punishments, but also allure them to virtue with rewards of honour. Therefore they set up in the market-place the images of notable men, and of such as have been great and bountiful benefactors to the commonwealth, for the perpetual memory of their good acts: and also that the glory and renown of the ancestors may stir and provoke their posterity to virtue. He that inordinately and ambitiously desireth promotions is left all hopeless for ever attaining any promotion as long as he liveth.

They live together lovingly. For no magistrate is either haughty or fearful. Fathers they be called, and like fathers they use themselves. The citizens (as it is their duty) willingly exhibit unto them due honour without any compulsion. Nor the prince himself is not known from the other by princely apparel, or a robe of state, nor by a crown or diadem royal, or cap of maintenance, but by a little sheaf of corn carried before him. And so a taper of wax is borne before the bishop, whereby only he is known.

They have but few laws. For to people so instructed and instituted very few do suffice. Yea, this thing they chiefly reprove among other nations, that innumerable books of laws, and expositions upon the same be not sufficient. But they think it against all right and justice that men should be bound to those laws, which either be in number more than be able to be read, or else blinder and darker than that any man can well understand them.

Furthermore they utterly exclude and banish all attorneys, proctors, and sergeants at the law, which craftily handle matters, and subtly dispute of the laws. For they think it most meet that every man should plead his own matter, and tell the same tale before the judge that he would tell to his man of law. So shall there be less circumstance of words, and the truth shall sooner come to light, whilst the judge with a discreet judgment doth weigh the words of him whom no lawyer hath instructed with deceit, and whilst he helpeth and beareth out simple wits against the false and malicious circumventions of crafty children.* This is hard to be observed in other countries, in so infinite a number of blind and intricate laws.

But in Utopia every man is a cunning lawyer. For (as I said) they have very few laws; and the plainer and grosser that any interpretation is, that they allow as most just. For all laws (say they) be made and published only to the intent, that by them every man should be put in remembrance of his duty. But the crafty and subtle interpretation of them (forasmuch as few can attain thereto) can put very few in that remembrance, whereas the simple, the plain, and gross meaning of the laws is open to every man. Else as touching the vulgar sort of the people, which be both most in number, and have most need to know their duties, were it not as good for them that no law were made at all, as when it is made, to bring so blind an interpretation upon it, that without great wit and long arguing no man can discuss it? To the finding out whereof neither the gross judgment of the people can attain, neither the whole life of them that be occupied in working for their livings can suffice thereto.

These virtues of the Utopians have caused their next neighbours and borderers, which live free and under no subjection (for the Utopians long ago have delivered many of them from tyranny), to take magistrates of them, some for a year, and some for five years'

* *children*: people.

space. Which, when the time of their office is expired, they bring home again with honour and praise, and take new again with them into their country.

These nations have undoubtedly very well and wholesomely provided for their commonwealths. For seeing that both the making and marring of the weal public doth depend and hang upon the manners of the rulers and magistrates, what officers could they more wisely have chosen than those which cannot be led from honesty by bribes (for to them that shortly after shall depart thence into their own country money should be unprofitable), nor yet be moved either with favour or malice towards any man, as being strangers, and unacquainted with the people? The which two vices of affection and avarice, where they take place in judgments, incontinent they break justice, the strongest and surest bond of a commonwealth. These people who fetch their officers and rulers from them, the Utopians call their fellows. And others to whom they have been beneficial, they call their friends.

As touching leagues, which in other places between country and country be so oft concluded, broken, and renewed, they never make none with any nation. For to what purpose serve leagues? say they. As though nature had not set sufficient love between man and man. And whoso regardeth not nature, think you that he will pass for words? They be brought into this opinion chiefly because that, in those parts of the world, leagues between princes be wont to be kept and observed very slenderly.

For here in Europe, and especially in these parts where the faith and religion of Christ reigneth, the majesty of leagues is everywhere esteemed holy and inviolable, partly through the justice and goodness of princes, and partly at the reverence and motion of the head bishops. Which like as they make no promise themselves, but they do very religiously perform the same, so they exhort all princes in any wise to abide by their promises, and them that refuse or deny so to do, by their pontifical power and authority they compel thereto. And surely they think well that it might seem a very reproachful thing, if in the leagues of them which by a peculiar name be called faithful, faith should have no place.

But in that new-found part of the world which is scarcely so far from us beyond the line equinoctial as our life and manners be dissident from theirs, no trust nor confidence is in leagues. But the

more and holier ceremonies the league is knit up with, the sooner it
is broken by some cavillation found in the words, which many times
of purpose be so craftily put in and placed, that the bands can never
be so sure nor so strong, but they will find some hole open to creep
out at, and to break both league and truth. The which crafty dealing,
yea, the which fraud and deceit, if they should know it to be practised
among private men in their bargains and contracts, they would
incontinent cry out at it with an open mouth and a sour countenance, as an offence most detestable, and worthy to be punished with
a shameful death; yea, even very they that advance themselves authors
of like counsel given to princes. Wherefore it may well be thought,
either that all justice is but a base and a low virtue, and which avaleth
itself far under the high dignity of kings, or, at the leastwise, that there
be two justices, the one meet for the inferior sort of people, going
afoot and creeping low by the ground, and bound down on every
side with many bands, because it shall not run at rovers. The other a
princely virtue, which like as it is of much higher majesty than the
other poor justice, so also it is of much more liberty, as to the which
nothing is unlawful that it lusteth after.

These manners of princes (as I said) which be there so evil keepers
of leagues, cause the Utopians, as I suppose, to make no leagues at all,
which perchance would change their mind if they lived here.
Howbeit they think that though leagues be never so faithfully
observed and kept, yet the custom of making leagues was very evil
begun. For this causeth men (as though nations which be separate
asunder, by the space of a little hill or a river, were coupled together
by no society or bond of nature) to think themselves born adversaries
and enemies one to another, and that it were lawful for the one to
seek the death and destruction of the other, if leagues were not. Yea,
and that after the leagues be accorded, friendship doth not grow and
increase, but the licence of robbing and stealing doth still remain, as
farforth as for lack of foresight and advisement in writing the words of
the league, any sentence or clause to the contrary is not therein
sufficiently comprehended.

But they be of a contrary opinion. That is, that no man ought to be
counted an enemy, which hath done no injury. And that the
fellowship of nature is a strong league; and that men be better and
more surely knit together by love and benevolence than by covenants
of leagues; by hearty affection of mind than by words.

Of Warfare

War or battle as a thing very beastly, and yet to no kind of beasts in so much use as to man, they do detest and abhor. And contrary to the custom almost of all other nations, they count nothing so much against glory, as glory gotten in war. And therefore though they do daily practise and exercise themselves in the discipline of war, and not only the men, but also the women upon certain appointed days, lest they should be to seek in the feat of arms, if need should require, yet they never go to battle, but either in the defence of their own country, or to drive out of their friends' land the enemies that have invaded it, or by their power to deliver from the yoke and bondage of tyranny some people that be therewith oppressed. Which thing they do of mere pity and compassion.

Howbeit they send help to their friends not ever in their defence, but sometimes also to requite and revenge injuries before to them done. But this they do not unless their counsel and advice in the matter be asked whiles it is yet new and fresh. For if they find the cause probable, and if the contrary part will not restore again such things as be of them justly demanded, then they be the chief authors and makers of the war. Which they do not only as oft as by inroads and invasions of soldiers preys and booties be driven away, but then also much more mortally when their friends' merchants in any land, either under the pretence of unjust laws, or else by the wresting and wrong understanding of good laws, do sustain an unjust accusation under the colour of justice.

Neither the battle which the Utopians fought for the Nephelogetes against the Alaopolitanes a little before our time was made for any other cause, but that the Nephelogete merchantmen, as the Utopians thought, suffered wrong of the Alaopolitanes, under the pretence of right. But whether it were right or wrong, it was with so cruel and mortal war revenged, the countries round about joining their help and power to the puissance and malice of both parties, that most flourishing and wealthy peoples, being some of them shrewdly shaken, and some of them sharply beaten, the mischiefs were not finished nor ended, until the Alaopolitanes at the last were yielded up as bondmen into the jurisdiction of the Nephelogetes. For the Utopians fought not this war for themselves. And yet the Nephelogetes before the war, when the Alaopolitanes flourished in wealth, were nothing to be compared with them.

So eagerly the Utopians prosecute the injuries done to their friends; yea, in money matters, and not their own likewise. For if they by covin or guile be wiped beside their goods, so that no violence be done to their bodies, they wreak their anger by abstaining from occupying with that nation until they have made satisfaction.

Not for because they set less store by their own citizens than by their friends, but that they take the loss of their friends' money more heavily than the loss of their own. Because that their friends' merchantmen, for as much as that they lose is their own private goods, sustain great damage by the loss. But their own citizens lose nothing but of the common goods, and of that which was at home plentiful and almost superfluous, else had it not been sent forth. Therefore no man feeleth the loss. And for this cause they think it too cruel an act to revenge that loss with the death of many, the incommodity of the which loss no man feeleth neither in his life, nor yet in his living.

But if it chance that any of their men in any other country be maimed or killed, whether it be done by a common or a private counsel, knowing and trying out the truth of the matter by their ambassadors, unless the offenders be rendered unto them in recompense of the injury, they will not be appeased, but incontinent they proclaim war against them. The offenders yielded, they punish either with death or with bondage.

They be not only sorry, but also ashamed to achieve the victory with bloodshed, counting it great folly to buy precious wares too dear. They rejoice and avaunt themselves if they vanquish and oppress their enemies by craft and deceit. And for that act they make a general triumph, and as if the matter were manfully handled, they set up a pillar of stone in the place where they so vanquished their enemies, in token of the victory. For then they glory, then they boast and crack that they have played the men indeed, when they have so overcome, as no other living creature but only man could, that is to say, by the might and puissance of wit. For with bodily strength (say they) bears, lions, boars, wolves, dogs, and other wild beasts do fight. And as the most part of them do pass us in strength and fierce courage, so in wit and reason we be much stronger than they all.

Their chief and principal purpose in war is to obtain that thing which, if they had before obtained, they would not have moved battle. But if that be not possible, they take so cruel vengeance of them which be in the fault, that ever after they be afraid to do the like. This is their chief and principal intent, which they immediately and first of all prosecute and set forward. But yet so, that they be more circumspect in avoiding and eschewing jeopardies, than they be desirous of praise and renown. Therefore immediately after that war is once solemnly denounced, they procure many proclamations signed with their own common seal to be set up privily at one time in their enemies' land, in places most frequented. In these proclamations they promise great rewards to him that will kill their enemies' prince, and somewhat less gifts, but them very great also, for every head of them whose names be in the said proclamations contained. They be those whom they count their chief adversaries, next unto the prince. Whatsoever is prescribed unto him that killeth any of the proclaimed persons, that is doubled to him that bringeth any of the same to them alive; yea, and to the proclaimed persons themselves, if they will change their minds and come in to them, taking their parts, they proffer the same great rewards with pardon, and surety of their lives.

Therefore it quickly cometh to pass that their enemies have all other men in suspicion, and be unfaithful and mistrusting among themselves one to another, living in great fear, and in no less jeopardy. For it is well known that divers times the most part of them (and especially the prince himself) hath been betrayed of them in whom they put their most hope and trust. So that there is no manner of act nor deed that gifts and rewards do not enforce men unto. And in rewards they keep no measure. But remembering and considering into how great hazard and jeopardy they call them, endeavour themselves to recompense the greatness of the danger with like great benefits. And therefore they promise not only wonderful great abundance of gold, but also lands of great revenues lying in most safe places among their friends. And their promises they perform faithfully without any fraud or covin.

This custom of buying and selling adversaries among other people is disallowed, as a cruel act of a base and a cowardish mind. But they in this behalf think themselves much praiseworthy, as who like wise men by this means despatch great wars without any battle or skirmish. Yea, they count it also a deed of pity and mercy, because that by the death of a few offenders the lives of a great number of innocents, as well of their own men as also of their enemies, be ransomed and saved, which in fighting should have been slain. For they do no less pity the base and common sort of their enemies' people than they do their own; knowing that they be driven and enforced to war against their wills by the furious madness of their princes and heads.

If by none of these means the matter go forward as they would have it, then they procure occasions of debate and dissension to be spread among their enemies. As by bringing the prince's brother, or some of the noblemen in hope to obtain the kingdom. If this way prevail not, then they raise up the people that be next neighbours and borderers to their enemies, and them they set in their necks under the colour of some old title of right, such as kings do never lack. To them they promise their help and aid in their war. And as for money they give them abundance, but of their own citizens they send to them few or none. Whom they make so much of, and love so entirely, that they would not be willing to change any of them for their adversaries' prince. But their gold and silver, because they keep it all for this only purpose, they lay it out frankly and freely; as who should live even as wealthy, if they had bestowed it every penny. Yea and besides their riches which they keep at home, they have also an infinite treasure abroad, by reason that (as I said before) many nations be in their debt. Therefore they hire soldiers out of all countries and send them to battle; but chiefly of the Zapoletes.

This people is five hundred miles from Utopia eastward. They be hideous, savage, and fierce, dwelling in wild woods and high mountains, where they were bred and brought up. They be of a hard nature, able to abide and sustain heat, cold, and labour, abhorring from all delicate dainties, occupying no husbandry nor tillage of the ground, homely and rude both in building of their houses and in their apparel, given unto no goodness, but only to the breeding and bringing up of cattle. The most part of their living is by hunting and stealing. They be born only to war, which they diligently and earnestly seek for. And when they have gotten it, they be wondrous glad thereof. They go forth of their country in great companies together, and whosoever lacketh soldiers, there they proffer their service for small wages. This is only the craft they have to get their living by. They maintain their life by seeking their death. For them whom with they be in wages they fight hardly, fiercely, and faithfully. But they bind themselves for no certain time. But upon this condition they enter into bonds, that the next day they will take part with the other side for greater wages, and the next day after that, they will be ready to come back again for a little more money. There be few wars thereaway, wherein is not a great number of them in both parties. Therefore it daily chanceth that any kinsfolk which were hired together on one part, and there very friendly and familiarly used themselves one with another, shortly after being separate in contrary parts, run one against another enviously and fiercely, and forgetting both kindred and friendship, thrust their swords one in another. And that for none other cause, but that they be hired of contrary princes for a little money. Which they do so highly regard and esteem, that they will easily be provoked to change parts for a halfpenny more wages by the day. So quickly they have taken a smack in covetousness. Which for all that is to them no profit. For that they get by fighting, immediately they spend unthriftily and wretchedly in riot.

This people fighteth for the Utopians against all nations, because they give them greater wages than any other nation will. For the Utopians like as they seek good men to use well, so they seek these evil and vicious men to abuse. Whom, when need requireth, with promises of great rewards they put forth into great jeopardies. From whence the most part of them never cometh again to ask their rewards. But to them that remain alive they pay that which they promised faithfully, that they may be the more willing to put themselves in like danger another time. Nor the Utopians pass not how many of them they bring to destruction. For they believe that they should do a very good deed for all mankind, if they could rid out of the world all the foul stinking den of that most wicked and cursed people.

Next unto these they use the soldiers of them for whom they fight. And then the help of their other friends. And last of all, they join to their own citizens. Among whom they give to one of tried virtue and prowess the rule, governance, and conduction of the whole army. Under him they appoint two others, which, while he is safe, be both private and out of office. But if he be taken or slain, the one of the other two succeedeth him, as it were by inheritance. And if the second miscarry, then the third taketh his room, lest that (as the chance of battle is uncertain and doubtful) the jeopardy or death of the captain should bring the whole army in hazard.

They choose soldiers, out of every city those which put forth themselves willingly. For they thrust no man forth into war against his will. Because they believe, if any man be fearful and faint-hearted of nature, he will not only do no manful and hardy act himself, but also be occasion of cowardness to his fellows. But if any battle be made against their own country, then they put these cowards (so that they be strong bodied) in ships among other bold-hearted men. Or else they dispose them upon the walls, from whence they may not fly. Thus what for shame that their enemies be at hand, and what for because they be without hope of running away, they forget all fear. And many times extreme necessity turneth cowardness into prowess and manliness.

But as none of them is thrust forth of his country into war against his will, so women that be willing to accompany their husbands in times of war be not prohibited or letted. Yea, they provoke and exhort them to it with praises. And in set field the wives do stand every one by their own husband's side. Also every man is compassed next about with his own children, kinsfolks, and alliance, that they, whom nature chiefly moveth to mutual succour, thus standing together, may help one another. It is a great reproach and dishonesty for the husband to come home without his wife, or the wife without her husband, or the son without his father. And therefore if the other part stick so hard by it that the battle come to their hands, it is fought with great slaughter and bloodshed, even to the utter destruction of both parts. For as they make all the means and shifts that may be to keep themselves from the necessity of fighting, or that they may despatch the battle by their hired soldiers; so when there is no remedy, but that they must needs fight themselves, then they do as courageously fall to it, as before, whilst they might, they did wisely avoid and refuse it. Nor they be not most fierce at the first brunt. But in continuance by little and little their fierce courage increaseth, with so stubborn and obstinate minds, that they will rather die than give back an inch. For that surety of living which every man hath at home being joined with no careful anxiety or remembrance how their posterity shall live after them (for this pensiveness oftentimes breaketh and abateth courageous stomachs), maketh them stout and hardy, and disdainful to be conquered. Moreover their knowledge in chivalry and feats of arms putteth them in a good hope. Finally the wholesome and virtuous opinions, wherein they were brought up even from their childhood, partly through learning, and partly through the good ordinances and laws of their weal public, augment and increase their manful courage. By reason whereof they neither set so little store by their lives, that they will rashly and unadvisedly cast them away; nor they be not so far in lewd and fond love therewith, that they will shamefully covet to keep them, when honesty biddeth leave them.

When the battle is hottest and in all places most fierce and fervent, a band of chosen and picked young men, which be sworn to live and die together, take upon them to destroy their adversaries' captain, whom they invade, now with privy wiles, now by open strength. At him they strike both near and far off. He is assailed with a long and a continual assault, fresh men still coming in the wearied men's places. And seldom it chanceth (unless he save himself by flying) that he is not either slain, or else taken prisoner, and yielded to his enemies alive.

If they win the field, they persecute not their enemies with the violent rage of slaughter. For they had rather take them alive than kill them. Neither they do so follow the chase and pursuit of their enemies, but they leave behind them one part of their host in battle array under their standards. In so much that if all their whole army be discomfited and overcome saving the rearward, and that they therewith achieve the victory, then they had rather let all their enemies escape than to follow them out of array. For they remember it hath chanced unto themselves more than once; the whole power and strength of their host being vanquished and put to flight, whilst their enemies rejoicing in the victory have persecuted them flying some one way and some another, a small company of their men lying in an ambush, there ready at all occasions, have suddenly risen upon them thus dispersed and scattered out of the array, and through presumption of safety unadvisedly pursuing the chase; and have incontinent changed the fortune of the whole battle, and, spite of their teeth wresting out of their hands the sure and undoubted victory, being a little before conquered, have for their part conquered the conquerors.

It is hard to say whether they be craftier in laying an ambush, or wittier in avoiding the same. You would think they intend to fly, when they mean nothing less. And contrariwise when they go about that purpose, you would believe it were the least part of their thought. For if they perceive themselves either overmatched in number, or closed in too narrow a place, then they remove their camp either in the night season with silence, or by some policy they deceive their enemies, or in the day-time they retire back so softly, that it is no less jeopardy to meddle with them when they give back than when they press on.

They fence and fortify their camp surely with a deep and a broad trench. The earth thereof is cast inward. Nor they do not set drudges and slaves awork about it. It is done by the hands of the soldiers themselves. All the whole army worketh upon it, except them that keep watch and ward in harness before the trench for sudden adventures. Therefore by the labour of so many a large trench closing in a great compass of ground is made in less time than any man would believe.

Their armour or harness which they wear is sure and strong to receive strokes, and handsome for all movings and gestures of the body, insomuch that it is not unwieldy to swim in. For in the discipline of their warfare among other feats they learn to swim in harness. Their weapons be arrows aloof, which they shoot both strongly and surely, not only footmen, but also horsemen. At hand strokes they use not swords but pole-axes, which be mortal, as well in sharpness as in weight, both for foins and down strokes. Engines for war they devise and invent wondrous wittily. Which when they be made they keep very secret, lest if they should be known before need require, they should be but laughed at and serve to no purpose. But in making them, hereunto they have chief respect, that they be both easy to be carried and handsome to be moved and turned about.

Truce taken with their enemies for a short time they do so firmly and faithfully keep, that they will not break it; no not though they be thereunto provoked. They do not waste nor destroy their enemies' land with foragings, nor they burn not up their corn. Yea, they save it as much as may be from being overrun and trodden down either with men or horses, thinking that it groweth for their own use and profit.

They hurt no man that is unarmed, unless he be a spy. All cities that be yielded unto them, they defend. And such as they win by force of assault, they neither despoil nor sack, but them that withstood and dissuaded the yielding up of the same, they put to death, the other soldiers they punish with bondage. All the weak multitude they leave untouched. If they know that any citizens counselled to yield and render up the city, to them they give part of the condemned men's goods. The residue they distribute and give freely among them whose help they had in the same war. For none of themselves taketh any portion of the prey.

But when the battle is finished and ended, they put their friends to never a penny cost of all the charges that they were at, but lay it upon their necks that be conquered. Them they burden with the whole charge of their expenses, which they demand of them partly in money to be kept for like use of battle, and partly in lands of great revenues to be paid unto them yearly for ever. Such revenues they have now in many countries, which by little and little rising of divers and sundry causes be increased above seven hundred thousand ducats by the year. Thither they send forth some of their citizens as lieutenants, to live there sumptuously like men of honour and renown. And yet this notwithstanding much money is saved, which cometh to the common treasury; unless it so chance that they had rather trust the country with the money. Which many times they do so long, until they have need to occupy it. And it seldom happeneth that they demand all. Of these lands they assign part unto them which at their request and exhortation put themselves in such jeopardies as I spake of before.

If any prince stir up war against them, intending to invade their land, they meet him incontinent out of their own borders with great power and strength. For they never lightly make war in their own country. Nor they be never brought into so extreme necessity as to take help out of foreign lands into their own island.

Of the Religions in Utopia

There be divers kinds of religion not only in sundry parts of the island, but also in divers places of every city. Some worship for God the sun; some the moon; some, some other of the planets. There be that give worship to a man that was once of excellent virtue or of famous glory, not only as God, but also as the chiefest and highest God. But the most and the wisest part (rejecting all these) believe that there is a certain godly power unknown, everlasting, incomprehensible, inexplicable, far above the capacity and reach of man's wit, dispersed throughout all the world, not in bigness, but in virtue and power. Him they call the father of all. To him alone they attribute the beginnings, the increasings, the proceedings, the changes, and the ends of all things. Neither they give any divine honours to any other than to him.

Yea, all the other also, though they be in divers opinions, yet in this point they agree altogether with the wisest sort, in believing that there is one chief and principal God, the maker and ruler of the whole world, whom they all commonly in their country language call Mithra. But in this they disagree, that among some he is counted one, and among some another. For every one of them, whatsoever that is which he taketh for the chief god, thinketh it to be the very same nature, to whose only divine might and majesty the sum and sovereignty of all things by the consent of all people is attributed and given.

Howbeit they all begin by little and little to forsake and fall from this variety of superstitions, and to agree together in that religion which seemeth by reason to pass and excel the residue. And it is not to be doubted, but all the other would long ago have been abolished, but that whatsoever unprosperous thing happened to any of them, as he was minded to change his religion, the fearfulness of people did take it, not as a thing coming by chance, but as sent from God out of heaven. As though the God, whose honour he was forsaking would revenge that wicked purpose against him.

But after they heard us speak of the name of Christ, of His doctrine, laws, miracles, and of the no less wonderful constancy of so many martyrs, whose blood willingly shed brought a great number of nations throughout all parts of the world into their sect, you will not believe with how glad minds they agreed unto the same; whether it were by the secret inspiration of God, or else for that they thought it nighest unto that opinion, which among them is counted the chiefest. Howbeit I think this was no small help and furtherance in the matter, that they heard us say, that Christ instituted among His all things common, and that the same community doth yet remain amongst the rightest Christian companies. Verily, howsoever it came to pass, many of them consented together in our religion, and were washed in the holy water of baptism.

But because among us four (for no more of us was left alive, two of our company being dead) there was no priest, which I am right sorry for, they being entered and instructed in all other points of our religion, lack only those sacraments which here none but priests do minister. Howbeit they understand and perceive them, and be very desirous of the same. Yea, they reason and dispute the matter earnestly among themselves, whether without the sending of a Christian bishop, one chosen out of their own people may receive the order of priesthood. And truly they were minded to choose one. But at my departure from them they had chosen none.

They also which do not agree to Christ's religion fear no man from it, nor speak against any man that hath received it. Saving that one of our company in my presence was sharply punished. He as soon as he was baptised, began against our wills, with more earnest affection than wisdom, to reason of Christ's religion, and began to wax so hot in his matter, that he did not only prefer our religion before all other, but also did utterly despise and condemn all other, calling them profane, and the followers of them wicked and devilish, and the children of everlasting damnation. When he had thus long reasoned the matter, they laid hold on him, accused him, and condemned him into exile, not as a despiser of religion, but as a seditious person, and a raiser up of dissension among the people. For this is one of the ancientest laws among them: that no man shall be blamed for reasoning in the maintenance of his own religion.

For King Utopus, even at the first beginning, hearing that the
inhabitants of the land were before his coming thither, at continual
dissension and strife among themselves for their religions; perceiving
also that this common dissension (whilst every several sect took
several parts in fighting for their country) was the only occasion of his
conquest over them all, as soon as he had gotten the victory, first of all
he made a decree, that it should be lawful for every man to favour
and follow what religion he would, and that he might do the best he
could to bring others to his opinion, so that he did it peaceably,
gently, quietly, and soberly, without hasty and contentious rebuking
and inveighing against others. If he could not by fair and gentle
speech induce them unto his opinion, yet he should use no kind of
violence, and refrain from displeasant and seditious words. To him
that would vehemently and fervently in this cause strive and contend
was decreed banishment or bondage.

This law did King Utopus make not only for the maintenance of
peace, which he saw through continual contention and mortal hatred
utterly extinguished, but also because he thought this decree should
make for the furtherance of religion. Whereof he durst define and
determine nothing unadvisedly, as doubting whether God desiring
manifold and divers sorts of honour, would inspire sundry men with
sundry kinds of religion. And this surely he thought a very unmeet
and foolish thing, and a point of arrogant presumption, to compel all
others by violence and threatenings to agree to the same that thou
believest to be true.

Furthermore, though there be one religion which alone is true, and
all others vain and superstitious, yet did he well foresee (so that the
matter were handled with reason and sober modesty) that the truth of
the own power would at the last issue out and come to light. But if
contention and debate in that behalf should continually be used, as
the worst men be most obstinate and stubborn, and in their evil
opinion most constant, he perceived that then the best and holiest
religion would be trodden underfoot and destroyed by most vain
superstitions, even as good corn is by thorns and weeds overgrown
and choked.

Therefore all this matter he left undiscussed, and gave to every man
free liberty and choice to believe what he would; saving that he
earnestly and straightly charged them, that no man should conceive
so vile and base an opinion of the dignity of man's nature as to think

that the souls do die and perish with the body, or that the world runneth at all adventures governed by no divine providence. And therefore they believe that after this life vices be extremely punished and virtues bountifully rewarded. Him that is of a contrary opinion they count not in the number of men, as one that hath avaled the high nature of his soul to the vileness of brute beasts' bodies: much less in the number of their citizens, whose laws and ordinances, if it were not for fear, he would nothing at all esteem. For you may be sure that he will study either with craft privily to mock, or else violently to break the common laws of his country, in whom remaineth no further fear than of the laws, nor no further hope than of the body. Wherefore, he that is thus minded is deprived of all honours, excluded from all offices, and reject from all common administrations in the weal public. And thus he is of all sorts despised, as of an unprofitable, and of a base and vile nature. Howbeit they put him to no punishment, because they be persuaded that it is in no man's power to believe what he list. No nor they constrain him not with threatenings to dissemble his mind, and show countenance contrary to his thought. For deceit and falsehood and all manners of lies, as next unto fraud, they do marvellously detest and abhor. But they suffer him not to dispute in his opinion, and that only among the common people. For else apart among the priests and men of gravity they do not only suffer, but also exhort him to dispute and argue, hoping that at the last that madness will give place to reason.

There be also other, and of them no small number, which be not forbidden to speak their minds, as grounding their opinion upon some reason, being in their living neither evil nor vicious. Their heresy is much contrary to the other. For they believe that the souls of brute beasts be immortal and everlasting. But nothing to be compared with ours in dignity, neither ordained nor predestinate to like felicity.

For all they believe certainly and surely that man's bliss shall be so great, that they do mourn and lament every man's sickness, but no man's death, unless it be one whom they see depart from his life carefully and against his will. For this they take for a very evil token, as though the soul being in despair and vexed in conscience, through some privy and secret forefeeling of the punishment now at hand, were afraid to depart. And they think he shall not be welcome to God, which, when he is called, runneth not to Him gladly, but is drawn by force and sore against his will. They, therefore, that see this kind of death, do abhor it, and them that so die they bury with sorrow and silence. And when they have prayed God to be merciful to the soul, and mercifully to pardon the infirmities thereof, they cover the dead corpse with earth.

Contrariwise all that depart merely and full of good hope, for them no man mourneth, but followeth the hearse with joyful singing, commending the souls to God with great affection. And at the last, not with mourning sorrow, but with a great reverence they burn the bodies. And in the same place they set up a pillar of stone with the dead man's titles therein graved. When they be come home they rehearse his virtuous manners and his good deeds. But no part of his life is so oft or gladly talked of as his merry death.

They think that this remembrance of the virtue and goodness of the dead doth vehemently provoke and enforce the living to virtue. And that nothing can be more pleasant and acceptable to the dead. Whom they suppose to be present among them when they talk of them, though to the dull and feeble eyesight of mortal men they be invisible. For it were an inconvenient thing that the blessed should not be at liberty to go whither they would. And it were a point of great unkindness in them to have utterly cast away the desire of visiting and seeing their friends, to whom they were in their lifetime joined by mutual love and amity. Which in good men after their death they count to be rather increased than diminished. They believe, therefore, that the dead be presently conversant among the quick, as beholders and witnesses of all their words and deeds. Therefore they go more courageously to their business as having a trust and affiance in such overseers. And this same belief of the present conversation of their forefathers and ancestors among them, feareth them from all secret dishonesty.

They utterly despise and mock soothsayings and divinations of things to come by the flight or voices of birds, and all other divinations of vain superstition, which in other countries be in great observation. But they highly esteem and worship miracles that come by no help of nature, as works and witnesses of the present power of God. And such they say do chance there very often. And sometimes in great and doubtful matters, by common intercession and prayers, they procure and obtain them with a sure hope and confidence and a steadfast belief.

They think that the contemplation of nature, and the praise thereof coming, is to God a very acceptable honour. Yet there be many so earnestly bent and affectioned to religion, that they pass nothing for learning, nor give their minds to any knowledge of things. But idleness they utterly forsake and eschew, thinking felicity after this life to be gotten and obtained by busy labours and good exercises. Some, therefore, of them attend upon the sick, some amend highways, cleanse ditches, repair bridges, dig turfs, gravel, and stones, fell and cleave wood, bring wood, corn, and other things into the cities in carts, and serve not only in common works, but also in private labours as servants, yea, more than bondmen. For whatsoever unpleasant, hard, and vile work is anywhere, from the which labour, loathsomeness, and desperation doth frighten others, all that they take upon them willingly and gladly, procuring quiet and rest to others, remaining in continual work and labour themselves, not upbraiding others therewith. They neither reprove other men's lives nor glory in their own. These men the more serviceable they behave themselves, the more they be honoured of all men.

Yet they be divided into two sects. The one is of them that live single and chaste, abstaining not only from the company of women, but also from eating of flesh, and some of them from all manner of beasts. Which utterly rejecting the pleasures of this present life as hurtful, be all wholly set upon the desire of the life to come by watching and sweating, hoping shortly to obtain it, being in the mean season merry and lusty. The other sect is no less desirous of labour, but they embrace matrimony, not despising the solace thereof, thinking that they cannot be discharged of their bounden duties towards nature without labour and toil, nor towards their native country without procreation of children. They abstain from no pleasure that doth nothing hinder them from labour. They love the flesh of four-footed beasts, because they believe that by that meat they be made hardier and stronger to work. The Utopians count this sect the wiser, but the other the holier. Which in that they prefer single life before matrimony, and that sharp life before an easier life, if herein they grounded upon reason they would mock them. But now forasmuch as they say they be led to it by religion, they honour and worship them. And these be they whom in their language by a peculiar name they call Buthrescas, the which word by interpretation signifieth to us men of religion or religious men.

They have priests of exceeding holiness, and therefore very few. For there be but thirteen in every city according to the number of their churches, saving when they go forth to battle. For then seven of them go forth with the army, in whose stead so many new be made at home. But the other at their return home again re-enter every one into his own place, they that be above the number, until such time as they succeed into the places of the others at their dying, be in the mean season continually in company with the bishop. For he is the chief head of them all.

They be chosen of the people, as the other magistrates be, by secret voices, for the avoiding of strife. After their election they be consecrated of their own company. They be overseers of all divine matters, orderers of religions, and as it were judges and masters of manners. And it is a great dishonesty and shame to be rebuked or spoken to by any of them for dissolute and incontinent living. But as it is their office to give good exhortations and counsel, so is it the duty of the prince and the other magistrates to correct and punish offenders, saving that the priests whom they find exceeding vicious livers, them they excommunicate from having any interest in divine matters. And there is almost no punishment among them more feared. For they run in very great infamy, and be inwardly tormented with a secret fear of religion, and shall not long escape free with their bodies. For unless they by quick repentance approve the amendment of their lives to the priests, they be taken and punished of the council as wicked and irreligious.

Both childhood and youth is instructed and taught of them. Nor they be not more diligent to instruct them in learning than in virtue and good manners. For they use with very great endeavour and diligence to put into the heads of their children, whilst they be yet tender and pliant, good opinions and profitable for the conservation of their weal public. Which, when they be once rooted in children, do remain with them all their life after, and be wondrous profitable for the defence and maintenance of the state of the commonwealth. Which never decayeth but through vices rising of evil opinions.

The priests, unless they be women (for that kind is not excluded from priesthood, howbeit few be chosen, and none but widows and old women), the men priests, I say, take to their wives the chiefest women in all their country. For to no office among the Utopians is more honour and pre-eminence given. Insomuch that if they commit any offence, they be under no common judgment, but be left only to God and themselves. For they think it not lawful to touch him with man's hand, be he never so vicious, which after so singular a sort was dedicated and consecrated to God as a holy offering.

This manner may they easily observe, because they have so few priests, and do choose them with such circumspection. For it scarcely ever chanceth that the most virtuous among virtuous, which in respect only of his virtue is advanced to so high a dignity, can fall to vice and wickedness. And if it should chance indeed (as man's nature is mutable and frail), yet by reason they be so few, and promoted to no might nor power but only to honour, it were not to be feared that any great damage by them should happen and ensue to the commonwealth. They have so rare and few priests, lest if the honour were communicated to many, the dignity of the order, which among them now is so highly esteemed, should run in contempt. Specially because they think it hard to find many so good as to be meet for that dignity, to the execution and discharge whereof it is not sufficient to be endued with mean virtues.

Furthermore these priests be not more esteemed of their own countrymen than they be of foreign and strange countries. Which thing may hereby plainly appear. And I think also that this is the cause of it. For whilst the armies be fighting together in open field, they a little beside, not far off, kneel upon their knees in their hallowed vestments, holding up their hands to heaven; praying first of all for peace, next for victory of their own part, but to neither part a bloody victory. If their host get the upper hand, they run into the main battle and restrain their own men from slaying and cruelly pursuing their vanquished enemies. Which enemies, if they do but see them and speak to them, it is enough for the safeguard of their lives. And the touching of their clothes defendeth and saveth all their goods from ravin and spoil.

This thing hath advanced them to so great worship and true majesty among all nations, that many times they have as well preserved their own citizens from the cruel force of their enemies, as they have their enemies from the furious rage of their own men. For it is well known that, when their own army hath recoiled, and in despair turned back, and run away, their enemies fiercely pursuing with slaughter and spoil, then the priests coming between have stayed the murder, and parted both the hosts. So that peace hath been made and concluded between both parties upon equal and indifferent conditions. For there was never any nation, so fierce, so cruel, and rude, but they had them in such reverence, that they counted their bodies hallowed and sanctified, and therefore not to be violently and unreverently touched.

They keep holy the first and the last day of every month and year, dividing the year into months, which they measure by the course of the moon, as they do the year by the course of the sun. The first days they call in their language Lynememes, and the last Trapememes, the which words may be interpreted, primifeast and finifeast, or else in our speech, first feast and last feast.

Their churches be very gorgeous, and not only of fine and curious workmanship, but also (which in the fewness of them was necessary) very wide and large, and able to receive a great company of people. But they be all somewhat dark. Howbeit that was not done through ignorance in building, but as they say, by the counsel of the priests. Because they thought that overmuch light doth disperse men's cogitations, whereas in dim and doubtful light they be gathered together, and more earnestly fixed upon religion and devotion; which because it is not there of one sort among all men, and yet all the kinds and fashions of it, though they be sundry and manifold, agree together in the honour of the divine nature, as going divers ways to one end, therefore nothing is seen nor heard in the churches, but that seemeth to agree indifferently with them all. If there be a distinct kind of sacrifice peculiar to any several sect, that they execute at home in their own houses. The common sacrifices be so ordered, that they be no derogation nor prejudice to any of the private sacrifices and religions.

Therefore no image of any god is seen in the church, to the intent it may be free for every man to conceive God by their religion after what likeness and similitude they will. They call upon no peculiar name of God, but only Mithra. In the which word they all agree together in one nature of the divine majesty whatsoever it be. No prayers be used but such as every man may boldly pronounce without the offending of any sect.

They come therefore to the church, the last day of every month and year, in the evening yet fasting, there to give thanks to God for that they have prosperously passed over the year or month, whereof that holy day is the last day. The next day they come to the church early in the morning, to pray to God that they may have good fortune and success all the new year or month which they do begin of that same holy day. But in the holy days that be the last days of the months and years, before they come to the church, the wives fall down prostrate before their husband's feet at home, and the children before the feet of their parents, confessing and acknowledging themselves offenders either by some actual deed, or by omission of their duty, and desire pardon for their offence. Thus if any cloud of privy displeasure was risen at home, by this satisfaction it is overblown, that they may be present at the sacrifices with pure and charitable minds. For they be afraid to come there with troubled consciences. Therefore if they know themselves to bear any hatred or grudge towards any man, they presume not to come to the sacrifices, before they have reconciled themselves and purged their consciences, for fear of great vengeance and punishment for their offence.

When they come thither, the men go into the right side of the church, and the women into the left side. There they place themselves in such order, that all they which be of the male kind in every household sit before the goodman of the house, and they of the female kind before the goodwife. Thus it is foreseen that all their gestures and behaviours be marked and observed abroad of them by whose authority and discipline they be governed at home. This also they diligently see unto, that the younger evermore be coupled with his elder, lest children being joined together, they should pass over that time in childish wantonness, wherein they ought principally to conceive a religious and devout fear towards God; which is the chief and almost the only incitation to virtue.

They kill no living beast in sacrifice, nor they think not that the merciful clemency of God hath delight in blood and slaughter, which hath given life to beasts to the intent they should live. They burn frankincense and other sweet savours, and light also a great number of wax candles and tapers, not supposing this gear to be anything available to the divine nature, as neither the prayers of men. But this unhurtful and harmless kind of worship pleaseth them. And by these sweet savours and lights, and other such ceremonies men feel themselves secretly lifted up, and encouraged to devotion with more willing and fervent hearts. The people weareth in the church white apparel. The priest is clothed in changeable colours. Which in workmanship be excellent, but in stuff not very precious. For their vestments be neither embroidered with gold nor set with precious stones. But they be wrought so finely and cunningly with divers feathers of fowls, that the estimation of no costly stuff is able to countervail the price of the work. Furthermore in these birds' feathers, and in the due order of them, which is observed in their setting, they say, is contained certain divine mysteries. The interpretation whereof known, which is diligently taught by the priests, they be put in remembrance of the bountiful benefits of God toward them; and of the love and honour which of their behalf is due to God; and also of their duties one toward another.

When the priest first cometh out of the vestry thus apparelled, they fall down incontinent every one reverently to the ground, with so still silence on every part, that the very fashion of the thing striketh into them a certain fear of God, as though He were there personally present. When they have lain a little space on the ground, the priest giveth them a sign for to rise. Then they sing praises unto God, which they intermix with instruments of music, for the most part of other fashions than these that we use in this part of the world. And like as some of ours be much sweeter than theirs, so some of theirs do far pass ours. But in one thing doubtless they go exceeding far beyond us. For all their music both that they play upon instruments, and that they sing with man's voice, doth so resemble and express natural affections, the sound and tune is so applied and made agreeable to the thing, that whether it be a prayer, or else a ditty of gladness, of patience, of trouble, of mourning, or of anger, the fashion of the melody doth so represent the meaning of the thing, that it doth wonderfully move, stir, pierce, and inflame the hearers' minds.

At the last the people and the priest together rehearse solemn prayers in words, expressly pronounced, so made that every man may privately apply to himself that which is commonly spoken of all. In these prayers every man recogniseth and knowledgeth God to be his maker, his governor, and the principal cause of all other goodness, thanking Him for so many benefits received at His hand. But namely that through the favour of God he hath chanced into that public weal which is most happy and wealthy, and hath chosen that religion which he hopeth to be most true. In the which thing if he do anything err, or if there be any other better than either of them is, being more acceptable to God, he desireth Him that He will of His goodness let him have knowledge thereof, as one that is ready to follow what way soever He will lead him. But if this form and fashion of a commonwealth be best, and his own religion most true and perfect, then he desireth God to give him a constant steadfastness in the same, and to bring all other people to the same order of living, and to the same opinion of God; unless there be anything that in this diversity of religions doth delight His unsearchable pleasure. To be short he prayeth Him, that after his death he may come to Him. But how soon or late that he dare not assign or determine. Howbeit, if it might stand with His majesty's pleasure, he would be much gladder to die a painful death and so to go to God, than by long living in worldly prosperity to be away from Him. When this prayer is said they fall down to the ground again and a little after they rise up and go to dinner. And the residue of the day they pass over in plays, and exercise of chivalry.

Now I have declared and described unto you, as truly as I could, the form and order of that commonwealth, which verily in my judgment is not only the best, but also that which alone of good right may claim and take upon it the name of a commonwealth or public weal. For in other places they speak still of the commonwealth. But every man procureth his own private gain. Here where nothing is private, the common affairs be earnestly looked upon. And truly on both parts they have good cause so to do as they do. For in other countries who knoweth not that he shall starve for hunger, unless he make some several provision for himself, though the commonwealth flourish never so much in riches? And therefore he is compelled even of very necessity to have regard to himself, rather than to the people, that is to say, to others.

Contrariwise there where all things be common to every man, it is not to be doubted that any man shall lack anything necessary for his private uses, so that the common storehouses and barns be sufficiently stored. For there nothing is distributed after a niggardish sort, neither there is any poor man or beggar. And though no man have anything, yet every man is rich. For what can be more rich than to live joyfully and merrily, without all grief and pensiveness, not caring for his own living, nor vexed or troubled with his wife's importunate complaints, nor dreading poverty to his son, nor sorrowing for his daughter's dowry? Yea they take no care at all for the living and wealth of themselves and all theirs, of their wives, their children, their nephews, their children's children, and all the succession that ever shall follow in their posterity. And yet besides this there is no less provision for them that were once labourers, and be now weak and impotent, than for them that do now labour and take pain.

Here now would I see, if any man dare be so bold as to compare with this equity, the justice of other nations. Among whom, I forsake God, if I can find any sign or token of equity and justice. For what justice is this, that a rich goldsmith, or an usurer, or, to be short, any of them, which either do nothing at all, or else that which they do is such that it is not very necessary to the commonwealth, should have a pleasant and a wealthy living, either by idleness, or by unnecessary business; when in the meantime poor labourers, carters, ironsmiths, carpenters, and ploughmen, by so great and continual toil, as drawing and bearing beasts be scant able to sustain, and again so necessary toil, that without it no commonwealth were able to continue and endure one year, should yet get so hard and poor a living, and live so wretched and miserable a life, that the state and condition of the labouring beasts may seem much better and wealthier? For they be not put to so continual labour, nor their living is not much worse, yea to them much pleasanter, taking no thought in the mean season for the time to come. But these silly poor wretches be presently tormented with barren and unfruitful labour. And the remembrance of their poor indigent and beggarly old age killeth them up. For their daily wages is so little, that it will not suffice for the same day, much less it yieldeth any overplus that may daily be laid up for the relief of old age.

Is not this an unjust and an unkind public weal, which giveth great fees and rewards to gentlemen, as they call them, and to goldsmiths, and to such other, which be either idle persons, or else only flatterers and devisers of vain pleasures; and of the contrary part maketh no gentle provision for poor ploughmen, colliers, labourers, carters, ironsmiths, and carpenters, without whom no commonwealth can continue? But after it hath abused the labours of their lusty and flowering age, at the last when they be oppressed with old age and sickness, being needy, poor, and indigent of all things, then forgetting their so many painful watchings, not remembering their so many and so great benefits, recompenseth and acquitteth them most unkindly with miserable death. And yet besides this the rich men not only by private fraud, but also by common laws, do every day pluck and snatch away from the poor some part of their daily living. So whereas it seemed before unjust to recompense with unkindness their pains that have been beneficial to the public weal, now they have to this their wrong and unjust dealing (which is yet a much worse point) given the name of justice, yea and that by force of a law.

Therefore, when I consider and weigh in my mind all these commonwealths which nowadays anywhere do flourish, so God help me, I can perceive nothing but a certain conspiracy of rich men procuring their own commodities under the name and title of the commonwealth. They invent and devise all means and crafts, first how to keep safely without fear of losing that they have unjustly gathered together, and next how to hire and abuse the work and labour of the poor for as little money as may be. These devices, when the rich men have decreed to be kept and observed under colour of the commonalty, that is to say, also of the poor people, then they be made laws.

But these most wicked and vicious men, when they have by their unsatiable covetousness divided among themselves all those things, which would have sufficed all men, yet how far be they from the wealth and felicity of the Utopian commonwealth? Out of the which, in that all the desire of money with the use thereof is utterly secluded and banished, how great a heap of cares is cut away ! How great an occasion of wickedness and mischief is plucked up by the roots ! For who knoweth not that fraud, theft, ravin, brawling, quarrelling, brabbling, strife, chiding, contention, murder, treason, poisoning, which by daily punishments are rather revenged than refrained, do die when money dieth? And also that fear, grief, care, labours, and watchings do perish even the very same moment that money perisheth? Yea poverty itself, which only seemed to lack money, if money were gone, it also would decrease and vanish away.

And that you may perceive this more plainly, consider with yourselves some barren and unfruitful year, wherein many thousands of people have starved for hunger. I dare be bold to say, that in the end of that penury so much corn or grain might have been found in the rich men's barns, if they had been searched, as being divided among them whom famine and pestilence then consumed, no man at all should have felt that plague and penury. So easily might men get their living, if that same worthy princess Lady Money did not alone stop up the way between us and our living, which in God's name, was very excellently devised and invented, that by her the way thereto should be opened. I am sure the rich men perceive this, nor they be not ignorant how much better it were to lack no necessary thing, than to abound with overmuch superfluity; to be rid out of innumerable cares and troubles, than to be besieged and encumbered with great riches.

And I doubt not that either the respect of every man's private commodity, or else the authority of our Saviour Christ (which for His great wisdom could not but know what were best, and for His inestimable goodness could not but counsel to that which He knew to be best) would have brought all the world long ago into the laws of this weal public, if it were not that one only beast, the princess and mother of all mischief, Pride, doth withstand and let it. She measureth not wealth and prosperity by her own commodities, but by the misery and incommodities of others, she would not by her goodwill be made a goddess, if there were no wretches left, over whom she might, like a scornful lady, rule and triumph, over whose miseries her felicities might shine, whose poverty she might vex, torment, and increase by gorgeously setting forth her riches. This hellhound creepeth into men's hearts, and plucketh them back from entering the right path of life, and is so deeply rooted in men's breasts that she cannot be plucked out.

This form and fashion of a weal public, which I would gladly wish unto all nations, I am glad yet that it hath chanced to the Utopians, who have followed those institutions of life, whereby they have laid such foundations of their commonwealth, as shall continue and last not only wealthily, but also, as far as man's wit may judge and conjecture, shall endure for ever. For, seeing the chief causes of ambition and sedition, with other vices, be plucked up by the roots, and abandoned at home, there can be no jeopardy of domestic dissension which alone hath cast under foot and brought to naught the well-fortified and strongly defended wealth and riches of many cities. But forasmuch as perfect concord remaineth, and wholesome laws be executed at home, the envy of all foreign princes be not able to shake or move the empire, though they have many times long ago gone about to do it, being evermore driven back.

Thus when Raphael had made an end of his tale, though many things came to my mind which in the manners and laws of that people seemed to be instituted and founded of no good reason, not only in the fashion of their chivalry, and in their sacrifices and religions, and in other of their laws, but also, yea, and chiefly, in that which is the principal foundation of all their ordinances, that is to say, in the community of their life and living, without any occupying of money, by the which thing only all nobility, magnificence, worship, honour, and majesty, the true ornaments and honours, as the common opinion is, of a commonwealth, utterly be overthrown and destroyed; yet because I knew that he was weary of talking, and was not sure whether he could abide that anything should be said against his mind; specially remembering that he had reprehended this fault in others, which be afraid lest they should seem not to be wise enough, unless they could find some fault in other men's inventions; therefore I praising both their institutions and his communication, took him by the hand, and led him in to supper, saying that we would choose another time to weigh and examine the same matters, and to talk with him more at large therein. Which would God it might once come to pass. In the meantime, as I cannot agree and consent to all things that he said, being else without doubt a man singularly well learned, and also in all worldly matters exactly and profoundly experienced; so must I needs confess and grant that many things be in the Utopian weal public which in our cities I may rather wish for than hope after.

THUS ENDETH THE AFTERNOON'S TALK OF RAPHAEL
HYTHLODAY CONCERNING THE LAWS AND
INSTITUTIONS OF THE ISLAND OF UTOPIA.

A Metre of Four Verses in the Utopian Tongue

briefly touching as well the strange beginning as also the happy and wealthy continuance of the same commonwealth

Utopos ha Boccas peula chama polta chamaan.
Bargol he maglomi baccan soma gymnosophaon
Agrama gymnosophon labarem bacha bodamilomin.
Voluala barchin heman la lauoluala dramme pagloni.

Which verses the translator, according to his simple knowledge, and mean understanding in the Utopian tongue, hath thus rudely Englished.

My king and conqueror Utopus by name,
A prince of much renown and immortal fame,
Hath made me an isle that erst no island was,
Full fraught with worldly wealth, with pleasure
    and solace.
I, one of all other without philosophy,
Have shaped for man a philosophical city.
As mine I am nothing dangerous to impart,
So better to receive I am ready with all my heart.

A Short Metre of Utopia

*written by Anemolius, poet laureate,
and nephew to Hythloday by his sister*

Me Utopie cleped Antiquity,
Void of haunt and herboroughe,
Now am I like to Plato's city,
Whose fame flieth the world through.
Yea like, or rather more likely
Plato's plat to excel and pass.
For what Plato's pen hath platted briefly
In naked words, as in a glass,
The same have I performed fully,
With laws, with men, and treasure fitly.
Wherefore not Utopie, but rather rightly
My name is Eutopie: a place of felicity.

The Utopian Alphabet

As it appeared in the first edition of Utopia

VTOPIENSIVM ALPHABETVM. 13

a b c d e f g h i k l m n o p q r s t u x y

TETRASTICHON VERNACVLA VTO-
PIENSIVM LINGVA.

Vtopos ha Boccas peula chama.

polta chamaan

Bargol he maglomi baccan

foma gymnofophaon

Agrama gymnofophon labarem

bacha bodamilomin

Voluala barchin heman la

lauoluola dramme pagloni.

HORVM VERSVVM AD VERBVM HAEC
EST SENTENTIA.

Vtopus me dux ex non infula fecit infulam.
Vna ego terrarum omnium abfcȝ philofophia.
Ciuitatem philofophicam expreffi mortalibus.
Libenter impartio mea, non grauatim accipio meliora.

b 3

Glossary

abroad: in other places (not 'in foreign lands')

alliant: related

amplifications: logical term applied to rules governing words which undergo an extension of meaning in propositions

in aunters: in case

avaleth: debases

avoutry: adultery

brazen: brass

(sudden) brunt: at one blow, suddenly

cark: care

cautel: precaution

cavillation: quibble

chaffer: bargaining

cleped: called

commodious: (1) comfortable; (2) generous, accommodating

commonwealth: body politic, nation, community

covin: conspiracy, fraud

crafty: able, skilful, ingenious

cunning: knowledgeable, able

make dearth: raise the price

disposition: ordering, arrangement of subject-matter

dizzards: clowns

engines: contraptions, instruments

engross: buy up wholesale

excogitated: contrived

existimation: reputation

families: households

fantasy: inclination, desire

fardel: collection, bundle

foins: thrusts

fond: silly

forestall: buy up privately to enhance price

gallous: wicked

gyves: fetters

handsome: convenient

happed: covered

herboroughe: lodging

I forsake God: may I perish

impotent: weak

improved: attacked

incontinent: immediately

invention: subject-matter

javel: rogue

jet: strut

let another man of: hinder another man's

earnest let: grave hindrance

profitable let: business to detain one

lewd: ignorant, unlearned
line equinoctial: the Equator
loadstone: magnet

matter: material
mattock: agricultural pick
moveth to: attempts
murrain: disease

naughty: worthless
noyous: harmful

in open houses: from the rooftops
(have their) ordinary recourses: are occasional

passeth: takes care
physic: medicine
pilled: pillaged, plundered
plat: plan, sketch; *platted*: sketched
platform: ground plan
plays: games
polled: cropped
prescript: prescribed
privy beck: discreet nod
puissance: power; *puissant*: mighty
pulleyn: poultry

quean: harlot, tart

ravin: robbery
re-edify: rebuild
restrictions: logical term applied to rules governing words which signify less than normal in propositions

rudeness: lack of literary polish
(like a) rule of lead: pliable, easily bent
run at rovers: run wild
rush-bucklers: swashbucklers

school (adj.): academic
sickerly: surely
silly: pitiable
softly: gradually
solicitor: advocate (in general sense)
spill: destroy, ruin
spite of their teeth: despite their best efforts
states: dignitaries
stews: brothel
straightly: strictly, severely
strait rules: strict decrees
stripes: lashes
suppositions: logical term applied to the study of the semantic content of words in propositions

train: artifice

ure: practice, employment
usurer: moneylender

vulgar: uneducated

waxed: grown
weal public: community, body politic; see commonwealth
welding: use, exercise
wiped beside: cheated of
wittily: sagaciously, knowingly
wryed: distorted

Names

Achoriens:	from Greek *a* = not, and *chora*, land
Ademus:	from Greek *a* and *demos*, people
Alaopolitanes:	from Greek *aleios*, poor in lands (or *alaos*, blind) and *polis*, city
Amaurote:	from Greek *amauros*, dim, obscure
Anemolians:	from Greek *anemos*, wind: hence, 'empty', 'vain'
Anemolius:	from Greek *anemos*: hence 'windbag'
Anyder:	from Greek *anydros*, without water
Hythloday:	from Greek *hythlos*, trifles; and *daiein*, to distribute; or *daios*, skilled, knowing
Lynememes:	More wrote Cynememes: from Greek *kuōn*, dog, and *hemera*, day ('dog-day')
Macariens:	from Greek *makarios*, happy, blessed
Nephelogetes:	from Greek *nephele*, cloud
Philarch:	from Greek *phylon* and *archōn*, ruler of a tribe
Syphogrant:	from Greek *supheos*, a sty and *gerōn*, old man, elder: possibly a pun on 'steward'
Tranibor:	from Greek *thranos*, bench (or *tranos* = clear, plain) and *boros*, devouring: possibly a pun on 'bencher'
Trapememes:	from Greek *trepein*, to turn ('turning-day')
Zapoletes:	from Greek *za* (intensive) and *pōlein*, to sell (i.e. mercenaries)